# Studies in Public Choice



For other titles published in this series, go to
http://www.springer.com/series/6550

Praise for *Democratic Governance and Economic Performance*

Dino Falaschetti skillfully synthesizes key ideas from social choice theory, organizational economics, and interest group politics to challenge conventional wisdom about the benefits of democratic governance in organizations. This is an important book for policymakers who are working to reform the way financial institutions are regulated, and corporations are governed, in the wake of the great financial market collapse of 2008. (Margaret Blair, Vanderbilt Law)

The scope of "Democratic Governance and Economic Performance" is truly commendable. Falaschetti argues persuasively that well-intentioned legal and regulatory structures can often create as many problems as they solve, often destroying social wealth in the process. While legal scholars, economists, and political scientists have raised parts of these issues before in isolation, by addressing the topic from the ground up at both the theoretical and empirical levels, this book provides useful perspective to anyone interested in the relationship between governance institutions and firm performance (Jon Klick, Penn Law)

This insightful book shares with Madison's "Federalist #10" a concern for the potentially disruptive effects of "majority factions." In telecommunications regulation, insurance regulation, and monetary policy (among other areas), popular coalitions led by elected officials are tempted by short-term gains to take actions that distort long-term incentives for economic growth. Falaschetti reminds us that some of our most costly economic policies are the direct result of democratic responsiveness, while some of our most successful policies have come from institutions (e.g., the courts and the Fed) that have been designed to be insulated from such democratic pressures (Gary Miller, Washington University, Political Science)

Dino Falaschetti

# Democratic Governance and Economic Performance

## How Accountability Can Go Too Far in Politics, Law, and Business

Springer

Dino Falaschetti
College of Law
Florida State University
Tallahassee FL 32306-1601
USA
dfalaschetti@law.fsu.edu

ISBN 978-0-387-78706-0 e-ISBN 978-0-387-78707-7
DOI 10.1007/978-0-387-78707-7
Springer Dordrecht Heidelberg London New York

Library of Congress Control Number: 2009927125



Printed on acid-free paper

Springer is part of Springer Science+Business Media (www.springer.com)

*For my heroes, Mimi and Yondro*

# Preface

> Washington is broken. The system is rigged. Cronyism and corporate interests prevail over fairness and the best interests of the American people.[1]

Senator Edwards is not alone in observing a lack of accountability in America's democracy. Indeed, both popular and academic media offer considerable support for this sentiment. The popular *Cable News Network* (*CNN*) criticized "government, big business, and special interest groups" for enriching themselves at the expense of the common electorate and characterized elected offices as "accountability free zones" while arguing that "our government no longer works for us."[2] Important scholars like John Matsusaka have added weight to this type of argument. Building on Robert Erikson et al.'s (1993) measure of government quality as "the responsiveness of public policymaking to the preferences of the mass public", for example, Professor Matsusaka found evidence that "government responds more to powerful interests than the general public" (2006, p. 1).

Instead of evidencing an undesirable lack of accountability in governance, however, observations like these are also consistent with democratic influences being so strong that economic performance suffers as a consequence. This conclusion follows from evaluating the quality of governance not against the popular standard of what people say but against the more revealing standard of what they do. The results can be surprising, and not only argue against blanket calls for increased accountability but also suggest that accountability may have already become too strong in important areas of politics, law, and business. Attempting to strengthen democratic governance in cases like these risks a further weakening of economic performance.

Understanding this risk, and how institutional and organizational strategies can productively address it, should interest students and scholars who work at the intersection of social science and the law and can help professionals improve their own performance in policy, legal, and business settings. In short, democratic institutions

---

[1] Source: former Senator John Edwards during his candidacy for the Democrat party's 2008 Presidential nomination, http://johnedwards.com/news/speeches/20070726-economic-fairness/, accessed 23 October 2007.

[2] Quoted from, respectively, Dobbs (2006), Jack Cafferty's March 12, 2007 commentary from the "Cafferty File" on CNN's "The Situation Room", and the back cover of Cafferty (2007).

that are regularly applauded for aligning the actions of political, legal, and business agents with the preferences of their principals (e.g., campaign finance restrictions, competition laws and regulations, and shareholder access to the corporate ballot) can also facilitate the taking of economic output for strategic redistributions. And like more widely appreciated sources of political expropriation (e.g., powerful governance agents rather than principal constituents), this one also constrains a society's economic opportunities. Consequently, while democratic governance is frequently measured by the responsiveness of policy to the preferences of principals, institutions that tighten this responsiveness can instead reduce government quality when evaluated against the standard of economic performance.

This type of political risk regularly threatens economic performance and the frequency with which even the most advanced economies realize its adverse consequences may be considerable. Following the devastation of Hurricane Katrina in the United States, for example, political agents arguably responded to electoral pressure by expanding insurance coverage beyond the bounds for which constituent premiums were paid. In particular, protection against wind-related damages was allegedly expanded after the fact to cover flood-related losses. Moreover, this expansion appears to have served constituent preferences, as electorates subsequently rewarded political agents who pushed for the expansion and punished those who opposed it. Accountability may have come at the price of economic performance, however, as suppliers of important insurance services soon exited the market (Wilson 2007).

Electoral pressure to alleviate recent credit market stresses may also ultimately discourage productive economic activity. The US House of Representatives' proposed "Mortgage Reform and Anti-Predatory Lending Act", for example, would let delinquent borrowers sue lenders for underestimating borrowers' repayment ability (e.g., see Saft 2007). While addressing constituents' calls to serve consumers (rather than financial service firms), however, creating this litigation opportunity could very well weaken repayment incentives and thus further the reluctance of intermediaries to channel credit. Given the importance of financial intermediation to general economic performance (e.g., see Levine 1997), the adverse effects of too much accountability in cases like this could be quite large.

*Democratic Governance and Economic Performance* develops economic models and statistical evidence that confront these intuitions with social scientific methods, and in doing so, builds a case that democratic institutions at various levels of governance (e.g., federal, state, corporation) can generate similar risks. To be sure, the book does not argue that accountability *necessarily* weakens economic performance, but rather that *too much* can diminish performance, and is likely to have done so in applications where accountability is popularly characterized as lacking.

The theories and evidence produced here thus equip organizational strategists in politics, law, and business to develop more productive institutions for accountability. In particular, rather than simplistically treating accountability as desirable under *any* circumstance, policymakers, lawyers, and managers can do better by weighing the agency benefits of increased accountability against the distributional costs of institutions and organizational arrangements that favor principal stakeholders over more general economic performance. Evaluating accountability relative to the standard of what people get, in this sense, can ultimately do better at giving them what they want.

## A Note on Method

This book builds, from the ground up, a sound theory and evidence about a relationship that popularly rests on informal conjecture; that is, democratic governance, at various levels of social and economic organization, generally improves welfare. It starts by formally *modeling* the phenomenon of interest. Done well, this type of research design can yield more firmly grounded and robust conclusions than do less-scientific approaches and, as we will see in this case, point to important empirical regularities that might have otherwise remained hidden.

Even when they are done well, however, formal investigations of human sociality are sometimes dismissed with statements like "that's just a theory." But an inescapable condition is that *everything* we do rests (often implicitly) on "just a theory;" that is, necessarily incomplete accounts of the "real world" that guide our actions. Gravity is just a theory. But it carefully rationalizes enough of what is "real" to land spacecraft on Mars – a world that (at least initially) revealed its truths to us not through intimate experience but through personally detached, firmly grounded, and logically developed *theory*.

Now, most of us are not physicists. However, we do seem to use good-enough models of gravity to lift ourselves from chairs or descend stairs without falling. Likewise, we implicitly use models of inertia to decide when and how hard to use our brakes and thus stop ourselves from crashing into cars ahead of us. Examples like these could easily go on, but the point is we do not need doctoral degrees to succeed at what we do – we need, and comfortably use, models! The important question is not whether we should tackle the task at hand with a model but rather how we can be confident that our model is a "good" one.

What, then, counts as "good" in this context? Any model must have a starting point, an initial condition that cannot be tested (otherwise, the condition would not be a starting point). Our set of standards for a good model thus begins with requiring assumptions to be self-evident and, to the extent that our assumptions are not obvious from introspection, our conclusions should not be overly sensitive to them. Second, we will want any such conclusions to logically build on our assumptions. A transparent statement about our assumptions and a mathematical derivation of hypotheses from those assumptions can serve these objectives well. Finally, we will want our hypotheses to highlight something that is empirically important but not trivially obvious. In other words, we will want to evaluate our hypotheses against data, while being careful that our conclusions are robust to possible statistical artifacts. Success on each of these margins can then let us confidently go forward with our model, not only in the empirical application where it was tested but also in any application in which the theory's assumptions are salient.

## Overview of the Book

Ultimately, a good model simplifies a superficially complex reality so that we can better understand the fundamental forces that may be driving it. This understanding, in turn, is necessary (though certainly not sufficient, as we will see) to govern those forces in a manner that expands, rather than strategically distributes, economic opportunities. Part I of this book attempts to build such a model of how democratic governance influences economic performance. Part II, then, uses this model to make sense of applications in politics, law, and business, and highlights individually attractive strategies for strengthening performance through each of these governance levels.

### *Theory: What Should We Observe if Democratic Governance Weakens Economic Performance?*

Part I begins by developing a model of "pressure group politics." The idea here is that producers and consumers compete for policies that yield individually attractive, but socially inferior, distributions. Conventional wisdom warns us about producers that would naturally accumulate economic power or enjoy political advantages that can be leveraged to accumulate power. The flipside of that wisdom, however, is that similarly situated consumers would also favor themselves over the greater good. And in a model that consistently characterizes individuals as being self-interested, whether they are producers or consumers, this latter outcome becomes a logical possibility.

In addition to assuming that everyone is self-interested, however, the model of pressure group competition assumes that bargaining power does not change over the life of (perhaps implicit) contracts. But relaxing this assumption does not change our conclusion, that is, consumers, like producers, will renegotiate what were originally win-win bargains whenever they can get the upper hand. In both of these models, and others, the observable implication is the same – when governance mechanisms overly favor a group of individuals (any group!), the favored group enjoys an attractive distribution not from expanding economic opportunities in general but from taking at the expense of others.

The important question for this book, then, is whether this principled risk is empirically important. Conventional wisdom seems to agree that too much producer power is a widespread difficulty, and careful scholarly studies have found evidence of producers being problematic in this important regard. But this book's theory does not say that one group naturally wins over the other, at the expense of economic performance more generally. Rather, it implies that "who wins" is sensitive to the structure of underlying politico-legal institutions. Put simply, when democratic governance becomes too strong, it facilitates "taking" by the masses and thus discourages producers from "making" in the first place. Here, the distribution of economic benefits opposes that which gives rise to conventional concerns (i.e., concerns about overly favoring producers), but constrains general economic opportunities all the same.

## *Natural Experiments: State Telecom Sectors Offer Attractive Labs for Studying Politics, Law, and Economics*

This model appears to be "good" in the sense that conclusions logically build on self-evident assumptions and appear rather insensitive to assumptions that may not be as agreeable a priori. To further evaluate whether we have a "good" model, then, we must empirically evaluate its implications. Here we want to learn whether the model lets us see something that less-formal methods may have left undiscovered, for example, whether democratic governance can indeed weaken economic performance.

To conduct this type of investigation, we need to find a naturally occurring "experiment" or conditions that approach those of a controlled setting. The goal here is to build assurance that our empirical inference is really attributable to the relationships that our model hypothesizes, rather than a statistical artifact. Chapter 2 thus asks what type of economic sector offers a good "lab" for evaluating whether democratic governance weakens economic performance only in principle, or whether it has actually done so in consequential applications.

For a number of reasons, state-level US local exchange sectors offer an attractive "quasi-experimental" setting in this regard. Importantly, each sector shares the same federal rules, but also works with different democratic institutions across states. Some states preclude campaign contributions from regulated utilities, for example, giving consumers a stronger voice in policy deliberations on the margin. States also vary in whether they elect or appoint utility regulators as well as in how they register voters. This oftentimes independent variation in democratic institutions, coupled with statistical tools that help us move even closer to experimental conditions, facilitates comparisons (again, on the margin) of how sectors perform when they are "treated" with democratic governance.

## *Statistical Evidence: Democratic Governance Probably Went Too Far in At Least One Important Sector*

Results from this statistical exercise speak strongly against the conventional wisdom; that is, evaluated on several margins where democratic governance varies, local exchange sectors exhibit inferior performance when consumer electorates enjoy stronger policy influence. To be sure, this result does not imply that a strengthening of democratic governance always leads to inferior social outcomes. Rather, it says that accountability appears to have gone too far in at least one important economic sector (a sector where the effects of that influence are relatively easy to discern).

At the same time, these results do not imply that the risk of too much democracy is particular to the sector in which it was empirically evaluated. The telecommunications sector offers a relatively controlled setting in which to consider whether this principled risk might become practically important. Indeed, that sector receives formal treatment in this book because of its quasi-experimental properties, not because our theories are particular to the sector. The statistical analysis reported in Chapter 3 thus suggests that other sectors with similar fundamentals (e.g., policy processes that are sensitive to pressure-group politics) may also be at risk of having democratic governance go too far, even if those sectors are less amenable to a formal empirical investigation.

## *Implications for Political Bureaucracy, Competition Law, and Business Organization*

Part II of *Democratic Governance and Economic Performance* investigates how this type of political risk can be realized at different levels of governance (e.g., federal, state, corporate) and thus weaken performance in other substantively interesting areas. Chapter 4 looks at how qualitatively similar forces play out at the macro-governance level, where overly democratic governance can compromise the productivity of monetary, fiscal, and trade policy. Chapter 5 then looks at an intermediate level of governance, namely antitrust laws and competition policies that (externally) govern business activity, and finds that markets like that for catastrophic risk insurance may also be underperforming because governance receives too much democratic pressure. Finally, Chapter 6 applies the theory at a micro-level of governance, that is, corporate governance. There, we also discover serious risks of democracy going too far, especially with respect to growing pressures for corporate law to strengthen the voice of shareholders.

At each level of governance, this book's robust theory says that the conventional wisdom about democratic governance can be wrong, and its empirical evidence says that this risk has plausibly been realized in important applications. To reiterate an important point, it does not say that democratic governance can never improve matters. Rather, its conclusion is that democratic governance probably deserves a more balanced evaluation. To that end, Part II also sketches some ideas on how political, legal, and business entrepreneurs can do better for themselves by facilitating this more widely attractive, but not always expedient, approach.

Tallahassee, FL Dino Falaschetti

## References

Cafferty, Jack (2007). *It's Getting Ugly Out There*. Hoboken, New Jersey: John Wiley & Sons, Inc.

Dobbs, Lou (2006). *War on the Middle Class*. New York: Viking Adult.

Erikson, Robert S., Gerald C. Wright, and John P. McIver (1993). *Statehouse Democracy: Public Opinion, and Policy in the American States*. Cambridge, New York, and Melbourne: Cambridge University Press.

Falaschetti, Dino (2002a). Does partisan heritage matter? The case of the federal reserve. *Journal of Law, Economics, and Organization*, 18(2), 488–510.

Falaschetti, Dino (2002b). Golden parachutes: Credible commitments or evidence of shirking? *Journal of Corporate Finance*, 8(2), 159–178.
Falaschetti, Dino (2003a). Can latent groups influence policy decisions? The case of telecommunications policy. *Journal of Law, Economics, & Organization*, 19(1), 83–105.
Falaschetti, Dino (2003b). Credible commitments and investment: Does opportunistic ability or incentive matter? *Economic Inquiry*, 41(4), 660–674.
Falaschetti, Dino (2005). *Can Electoral Mobility Diminish Economic Performance? Evidence from the US Telecommunications Sector*. SSRN Working Paper, October 11. doi: 10.2139/ssrn.413583.
Falaschetti, Dino (2007). *Electoral Accountability and Consumer Monopsonists: Evidence from Elected vs. Appointed Regulators*. SSRN Working Paper, July 24. doi: 10.2139/ssrn.645401.
Falaschetti, Dino (2008). When deficits make sense. *Hoover Digest*, (3), 72–75.
Falaschetti, Dino (2009a). Shareholder democracy and corporate governance. Forthcoming in *Review of Banking and Financial Law*.
Falaschetti, Dino (2009b). Can lobbying prevent anticompetitive outcomes? Evidence on consumer monopsony in telecommunications. *Journal of Competition Law and Economics*, 4(4), 1065–1096.
Falaschetti, Dino and Gary Miller (2001). Constraining Leviathan: Moral hazard and credible commitment in constitutional design. *Journal of Theoretical Politics*, 13(4), 389–411.
Falaschetti, Dino and Gary Miller (2004). Constraining rational choice: Allocation versus efficiency and the origin of commitment problems. In Irwin Morris, Joe Oppenheimer, and Karol Soltan (Eds.), *Politics from Anarchy to Semocracy* (pp. 110–131). Palo Alto: Stanford Law and Politics.
Falaschetti, Dino and Michael J. Orlando (2008). *Money, financial intermediation, and governance*. Cheltenham, UK and Northhampton, MA: Edward Elgar Publishing.
Levine, Ross (1997). Financial development and economic growth: Views and agenda. *Journal of Economic Literature*, 35(2), 688–726.
Matsusaka, John (2006). *Institutions and Popular Control of Public Policy*. USC Center in Law, Economics and Organization Research Paper No. C06-14.
Saft, Stuart M. (2007). The anti-mortgage lending act. *Wall Street Journal*, November 10, A10.
Wilson, James Q. (2007). A real insurance fraud. *Wall Street Journal*, November 16, A21.

# Acknowledgments

This book builds on several previous works,[1] each of which received a careful (though not always agreeable) evaluation from scholars who were generous with their time and effort. Presentations of and correspondences about different parts of this book greatly benefited from the attention of Kurt Annen, Lee Benham, Marcus Berliant, Jamie Brown, Don Bruce, Randy Calvert, Marco Castañeda, Robert Crandall, Suzanne Falaschetti, Steve Fazzari, Rob Fleck, Norman Frohlich, Rick Geddes, Jonah Gelbach, Andy Hanssen, Shawn Humphrey, Simon Jackman, John Jackson, Ivan Jeliazkov, Phil Keefer, Dan Kessler, Jack Knight, Keith Krehbiel, Randy Kroszner, Krishna Ladha, Bill Lowry, Mathew McCubbins, Dick Meyer, Gary Miller, James Morley, John Nachbar, Roger Noll, John Nye, Erik O'Donoghue, Mary Olson, Joe Oppenheimer, Mike Orlando, Bob Parks, Steve Parsons, Rudy Santore, Norman Schofield, Suzanne Scotchmer, Itai Sened, Greg Sidak, James Snyder, Chris Stoddard, Craig Stroup, Rick Stroup, Joe Tonon, and Donald Wittman. Seminar participants were also very kind in helping the development of these arguments, including those at Cornell University, the Federal Reserve Bank of Kansas City, Florida State University, Michigan State University, Montana State University, NERA Economic Consultants (San Francisco), Tulane University, University of California at Berkeley, University of Guelph, University of Maryland, University of Tennessee, Vanderbilt University, Washington University, West Virginia University, Yale University, and numerous academic conferences. Finally, David Brady, Joy Kelley, and other scholars at the Hoover Institution provided generous helpings of hospitality and rich intellectual exchange while much of this manuscript was being written.

Florida State University
Tallahassee, FL, USA

Dino Falaschetti

[1] See Falaschetti (2002a, b, 2003a, b, 2005, 2007, 2008, 2009a, b), Falaschetti and Miller (2001, 2004), and Falaschetti and Orlando (2008).

# Contents

# About the Author

Dino Falaschetti (PhD, MBA, CPA) is Associate Professor of Law and Economics at the Florida State University College of Law, an associate professor (by courtesy) in the Departments of Economics and Political Science, Campbell National Fellow at Stanford University's Hoover Institution, and President of Economic Advisors, Inc., a business analytics and litigation support firm. Dr. Falaschetti previously served the White House as a senior economist for the President's Council of Economic Advisers (with responsibilities for regulation and financial services), held academic appointments at Montana State University, University of California at Berkeley, University of Tennessee, and Washington University in St. Louis, and managed a $1 billion money market portfolio and financial statement audit-engagements for a Fortune 100 conglomerate. He earned a PhD in economics from Washington University in St. Louis (with fields in political economy, economic theory, and industrial organization), an MBA with high honors from the University of Chicago (with concentrations in economics and finance), and a BS with distinction from Indiana University (with a major in accounting and work in depth in philosophy).

# Part I
# A General Theory and Statistical Evidence

# Chapter 1
# Theory

## What Should We Observe if Democratic Governance Weakens Economic Performance?

Across social science disciplines, scholars agree that electoral constituents receive poor policy treatment when their political agents lack accountability. V.O. Key's (1984 [1949]) seminal inquiry, for example, produced evidence that constituents receive inferior treatment when they lack ready access to voting in elections. Extending this early insight, Robert Fleck (1999, 2001) found that depression-era distributive policy favored high-turnout constituencies, whereas Timothy Besley and Robin Burgess (2002) developed related evidence on government responsiveness in India. Similarly, James Hamilton (1993) reported that politically active North Carolinians faced a significantly reduced probability of having hazardous waste facilities expanded within their counties. In each case, democratic governance appears to have reduced political agency costs, at least for constituents to which relevant institutions encouraged accountability.

Perhaps it is this appearance that motivates democracy advocates to argue that increased accountability to electoral principals generally expands social welfare. Prominent organizations such as the Institute for Democracy and Electoral Assistance (IDEA), for example, characterize mechanisms that would increase electoral participation as being "dominant" – actions that are best under any conditions.[1] The International Foundation for Electoral Systems (IFES) similarly offers an unqualified assessment of participation's capacity to produce "government responsiveness and accountability."[2]

Popular media frequently concur, such as the *Wall Street Journal*'s applause for California voters who told "the political elite who's boss" and thus took the state's economy on a "marked turn for the better" (Power to the people 2004). Even more, the largest academic society for political scientists, American Political Science Association (APSA), announced a research award for "concrete contributions to solving social problems", a major theme of which was *Promoting Democracy*.[3]

---

[1]The IDEA conference on "Building Electoral Participation" is illustrative – see http://idea.int/, accessed on 31 July 2003.

[2]See, for example, http://www.ifes.org/civil.html, accessed on 4 December 2008.

[3]Source H-PolMeth Discussion Network. Available at http://www.h-net.org/. Accessed 6 July 2004 (emphasis added).

D. Falaschetti, *Democratic Governance and Economic Performance*, Studies in Public Choice 14, DOI 10.1007/978-0-387-78707-7_1,

However, these advocates may be reaching beyond the bounds of what we know from received scholarship. Importantly, that research tends to evaluate the *distributional* consequences of democratic governance within a set of electoral constituents. As such, it cannot (and was not intended to) explicitly address the relationship between democratic governance and economic performance, where performance is more immediately concerned with the "size of the pie" (as well as the growth of and fluctuations in that size). Appreciating this distinction is important since, while popular accounts tend to view "responsiveness and accountability" as strictly desirable properties of polities, decreasing the cost of politician–electorate agencies (i.e., strengthening democratic governance) can shrink a society's set of economic opportunities.

This chapter shows that this proposition creates a robust and readily observable implication; that is, if electoral accountability enhances economic performance, then proxies for accountability and output should share a positive relationship. Evidence developed in the rest of this book (both formal and informal), however, opposes this implication; that is, output in important economic sectors appears to decrease considerably when electoral principals can more strongly influence their democratic agents. Moreover, this normative inference (i.e., accountability can *weaken* economic performance) appears rather insensitive to modeling assumptions, and the empirical relationship on which it draws does not show itself to be a statistical artifact.

## 1.1 Output, Not Price, Reflects Economic Performance

### *1.1.1 An Informal Model of Pressure-Group Politics*

The potential for democratic governance to weaken economic performance, and the observable implication of having realized this potential, readily emerges from models of pressure-group politics – models that have helped address related questions in political economy and law and economics research. In these models, influential producers create benefits for themselves at the expense of economic performance more generally by encouraging politicians to increase prices toward their monopoly level. Sam Peltzman (1976) recognized, however, that the cost of transacting in political markets (e.g., time and effort to measure policy favors and enforce implicit contracts over them) will preclude dominant producers from completely "capturing" political agents – allowing for perhaps considerable inefficiencies but precluding extreme monopoly outcomes.[4] In cases like this, electoral pressure can improve economic performance by productively weighing against prices rising above their competitive levels.

[4] Arthur Denzau and Michael Munger (1986) developed a related conclusion from a model where competition between lobbying firms creates forces that discourage complete capture.

In addition to mitigating the well-known problem of regulatory capture, however, electoral pressure can *reverse* it. Here, just as concentrated producers can encourage politicians to sacrifice an economy's "total surplus" in return for favorable distributions, influential electorates can encourage politicians to sacrifice total surplus to expand consumer surplus.[5]

Fig. 1.1 illustrates how democratic governance can either expand general economic opportunities or shrink those opportunities in favor of distributions that are even more consumer friendly. It also highlights how these very different performance (but not distributional) effects can make themselves evident in how output (not price) responds to increased consumer pressure.

To observe this distinction, consider the monopoly price in Fig. 1.1 (P_monopolist), and notice that by increasing the political drag on this price, a strengthening of consumers' policy-influence expands total surplus. Indeed, as this influence begins to grow, price decreases from $P_{\text{monopolist}}$ to $P_{\text{competitive}}$ and output increases from $Q_{\text{anticompetitive}}$ to $Q_{\text{competitive}}$. This increase in quantity, in turn, is

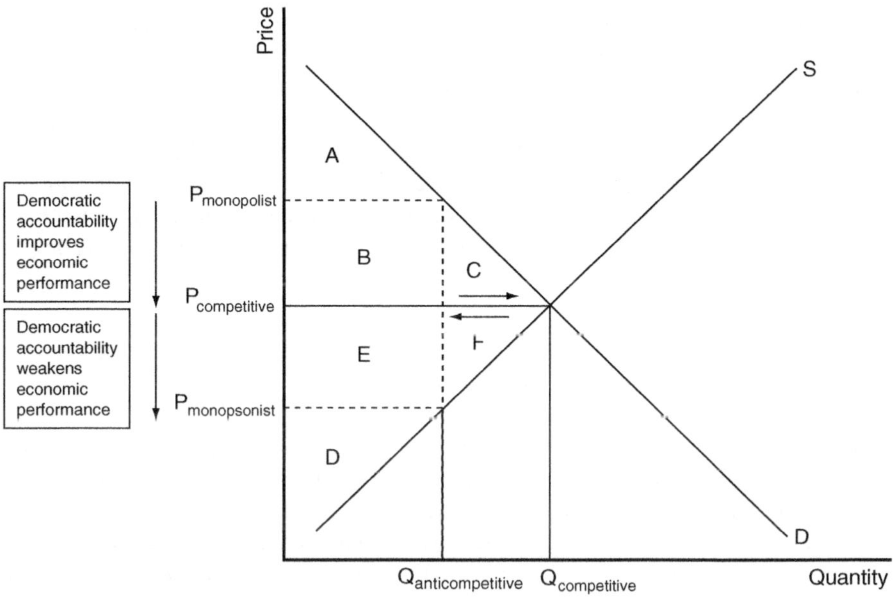


**Fig. 1.1** Economic distribution and performance in a model of pressure group politics

[5]By total surplus, we mean the sum of consumers' benefit from purchasing a good or service at a price below their willingness to pay and producers' benefit from selling a good or service above their willingness to supply. Graphically, in Fig. 1.1, total surplus equals the sum of the areas below the demand curve and above a given price (consumer surplus) and above the supply curve and below that price (producer surplus). Note that this measure of economic performance reaches its maximum (the size of the pie is greatest) when competition exhausts all mutually beneficial trades and thus extinguishes the "deadweight loss" triangles C and F.

associated with both a transfer of surplus from producers to consumers (represented by the area of rectangle B) and an expansion of total surplus (represented by the area of triangles C and F).

But consumers in this model do not want to stop pressing their democratic influence when price reaches its competitive level. Rather, they can do better by taking even more surplus from producers. But here, the redistribution weakens economic performance more generally, creating (rather than mitigating) a "deadweight loss" (represented by the area of triangles C and F). Indeed, by pushing price to its monopsony level ($P_{\text{monopsony}}$), consumers maximize their own surplus, taking the surplus that producers would have enjoyed in a competitive outcome (represented by rectangle E) while foregoing a relatively small portion of the surplus they would have realized at the competitive outcome (represented by the area of triangle C).

The welfare loss to society in this case can be just as large as the loss from a monopoly outcome – whether democratic governance is maximally weak or strong, society loses the surplus represented by the area of triangles C and F. At least in principle, democratic governance can go too far by benefitting consumers at the expense of general economic opportunities, rather than in a manner that expands total surplus.[6]

To answer the question in the title of this chapter, then, we should see evidence of output decreasing when democratic governance weakens economic performance. Importantly, while popular accounts, and even competition policy deliberations, focus on prices as a measure for economic performance,[7] it is quantity in this model that contains information about total welfare. And as the remainder of this chapter shows, this implication exhibits considerable robustness to the pressure-group model's assumptions.

## *1.1.2 A Formal Check on Our Intuition*

As Fig. 1.1 illustrates, our competing pressure-group model implies that whether restrictions encourage economies to approach or overshoot efficient outcomes can be observed in how output relates to electoral accountability. To develop this insight more carefully, let us examine a political agent that takes as its objective the maximization of an economy's total surplus, subject to political influence, as follows:

$$\max_{P} \{\alpha \times \mathit{Consumer\ Surplus} + (1-\alpha) \times \mathit{Producer\ Surplus}\} \tag{1.1}$$

[6]Thomas Lyon (2003) developed a similar insight to evaluate how the migration of regulatory authority from the municipal- to state-level may have strengthened regulatory commitments.

[7]See, for example, Joseph Pereira's (2008a,b) reports on a recent Supreme Court decision (and subsequent political backlash) that minimum-pricing contracts are not per se anticompetitive.

where

$$Consumer\ Surplus = \int_0^{Q(P)} Q_d(x)\, dx - P \cdot Q(P) \tag{1.2}$$

$$Producer\ Surplus = P \cdot Q(P) - \int_0^{Q(P)} Q_s(x) dx \tag{1.3}$$

$$Q_d(P) = \overline{P} - P \tag{1.4}$$

$$Q_s(P) = P \tag{1.5}$$

$$Q(P) = \min\{Q_d(P), Q_s(P)\} \tag{1.6}$$

and $\alpha \in [0,1]$ measures the strength of democratic governance (i.e., $\alpha = 1$ means that political institutions only let consumer electorates (as opposed to producer lobbyists) influence policy). This problem essentially pits consumers against producers in a "menu auction" game similar to that of Douglas Bernheim and Michael Whinston (1986). In games like this one, political agents completely allocate a fixed "prize" (e.g., $P$) between competing interests, and interests attempt to influence this allocation by credibly presenting to agents "political support menus" (i.e., lists of support that groups supply as a function of agents' feasible actions). Distribution of the "prize" thus depends on bidders' relative capacity to produce support, represented here by the parameter $\alpha$.[8]

Whether increasing consumer-accountability improves economic performance can be seen in how it relates to equilibrium quantity.[9] If the supply curve constrains equilibrium quantity, for example, then regulators choose prices according to the following rule:

$$P(\alpha) = \left(\frac{\alpha}{4\alpha - 1}\right)\overline{P} \tag{1.7}$$

Consequently, as consumer-accountability increases from $\alpha = 1/2$ to $\alpha = 1$,[10] equilibrium quantity decreases from $\bar{P}/2$ to $\overline{P}/3$, and total surplus shrinks from its maximum competitive level of $\overline{P}^2/4$ to its inferior consumer-monopsonist level

[8]This dependence is also evident in Gary Becker's (1983) model of pressure group competition.

[9]Peltzman (1976) argued that the cost of transacting in political markets limits the gains of "dominant groups." Applied to our current framework, this limit implies that the parameter $\alpha$ will not *rest* at either of its extreme values (i.e., $\alpha \neq 0$ or 1, although Peltzman's reference to the competitive outcome as a "benchmark" and corresponding reference to equilibrium (regulated) prices and quantities being read off of demand curves imply that he considered $\alpha = 0.5$ as an effective maximum). Our objective in examining the related problem (1.1) is to facilitate a more general normative investigation of electoral accountability by making transparent the observable implications of *changing* $\alpha$.

[10]The constraint $Q(P) = Q_s(P)$ defines rule (Equation 1.7)'s domain as the interval $\alpha \in (1/2, 1)$.

of $\bar{P}^2/6$. This relationship makes observable an implication of the hypotheses of Richard Schmalensee (2004, 1) and Mark Armstrong and David Sappington (2006, 331) that regulation's objective is consumer surplus, not overall economic welfare.

But because producers and consumers symmetrically enter this model, increasing consumer pressure can also increase total surplus, and this influence makes itself observable via an increase in equilibrium quantity. Whether increasing political accountability to consumer electorates expands total surplus thus depends in this model on whether it discourages regulatory capture on behalf of producers or facilitates that on behalf of consumers.

## 1.2 Robustness to Assumptions

Our pressure-group model offers clear observable implications for how democratic governance can influence economic performance. Because conclusions of formal empirical results from Chapter 3 (as well as informal results developed later in Part 2 of this book) build on this relationship, considering its sensitivity to modeling assumptions is important.[11] This section therefore examines how governance relates to performance in models that focus on other salient features of many empirical settings, including those that are germane to the local exchange and other sectors that we will evaluate in subsequent chapters.

### *1.2.1 What if Policy Credibility Is Important?*

Our model of pressure-group politics assumes that the producers' supply curve is upward-sloping; that is, the cost of production increases with quantity supplied. But what if the production process requires a considerable investment before it can get started? In common cases like this one, the supply curve can be relatively flat; that is, after initially sinking resources into the production process, the marginal cost of production is relatively small.[12] Here, the political risk that electorates pose is not so much inefficiently "taking" surplus from producers, as it is opportunistically renegotiating what may have started as mutually beneficial agreements.[13]

Following Douglass North and Barry Weingast (1989), contributors to the "institutions and commitment" literature characterized this problem as a fundamental

---

[11] Edward Leamer (1985) prominently called attention to this importance.

[12] Looking forward to our formal empirical examination, if we define quantity as an option for households to connect to the telecommunications network, then marginal costs plausibly increase with quantity; e.g., the physical distance over which local exchange service producers and subscribers must connect increases with additional subscribers. In this case, the supply curve slopes upward as in our pressure group model. If, instead, quantity refers to exercised options (e.g., calling minutes), then marginal (but not average) costs may be negligible.

[13] Finn Kydland and Edward Prescott (1977) developed a seminal model of this type of opportunism.

political obstacle to productive economic activity.[14] The inelasticity of supply from sunk investments makes capital levies an "optimal taxation" mechanism. But, this feature also weakens commitments against expropriating output that eventually comes from those investments, and thus discourages the productive employment of immobile resources in the first place (e.g., landline connections to telecommunications networks). Absent institutions that facilitate commitment, even surplus-maximizing political agents, will thus follow strategies that induce inferior economy-wide outcomes.

#### 1.2.1.1 Campaign Contributions Give Producers a "Voice" in Protecting Their Rights, and Thus Create a Productive Alternative to "Exiting" the Economy

Moving from a static to dynamic analytical framework, democratic governance can weaken economic performance by silencing a potentially productive "voice" from producers. Institutions such as campaign finance restrictions, for example, can leave producers with only the action of "exit" to protest undesirable political outcomes (Hirschman 1970), but exit opportunities for those who made hard-to-reverse investments are (by definition) unattractive. Anticipating such a weak ex post bargaining position, investors will shy away from sinking resources into production processes in the first place.

While decidedly undemocratic, then, an allowance for campaign contributions from non-voters can strengthen commitments against such opportunism, and thus act as a productive check on consumer pressures. The idea here is that political agents will be less eager to expropriate the product of sunk investments (on behalf of electoral principals) if the endgame is a campaign contribution (rather than an election). Withholding campaign contributions in dynamic settings can let producers "punish" regulators that opportunistically redistribute output from sunk investments and can thus strengthen commitments to efficiency-enhancing policies. It can also strengthen the protection of "property interests" by discouraging political redistributions between shareholding and non-shareholding electoral members (Sidak 2001).[15]

Nicolas Marceau and Michael Smart (2003), among others, formalized this intuition, developing a model where the capital levy problem is less threatening when producers can financially support (i.e., "lobby") political agents. Michelle Garfinkel and Jaewoo Lee (2000, p. 650) offered a similar insight, concluding that "reforms to limit [lobbying] may aggravate the credibility problem." This implication emerges

[14]See, for example, Levy and Spiller (1994), Acemoglu et al. (2001), Rodrik et al. (2002), Stasavage (2002), and Falaschetti (2003b).

[15]Sidak (2001, p. 747) argued that giving producers (corporations, in particular) a voice in policy deliberations is "significant" since "the repudiation of substantive due process, the decline of the Takings and Contract Clauses since the New Deal, and the simultaneous rise of the administrative state as a regulator of economic activity have made it increasingly difficult for individuals to defend their property against expropriation by the state."

from owners of sunk capital maintaining a relatively high willingness to pay for favorable policy. Understanding that rents from mobile capital are ephemeral, associated investors will rationally exert little in the way of lobbying effort, since that effort's product would be non-excludable. But, benefits from policies that favor immobile capital are relatively durable, and thus endow sunk capitalists with a superior lobbying technology. This superiority, in turn, discourages political agents from setting taxes in accord with adjustment costs. In cases like this, making governance more democratic (say, by tightening campaign finance restrictions) weakens this protection against investors having to bear the burden of opportunistic capital levies and can thus shrink a society's economic capacity.

#### 1.2.1.2 Unelected Regulators Face Less Pressure from Consumer Monopsonists and Can More Credibly Protect Producer Rights

Absent institutions that facilitate commitment, even surplus-maximizing political agents will follow strategies that induce inferior equilibria (where "inferior", again, is reflected in output levels). As the preceding section argued, institutions like an allowance for campaign contributions can improve economic performance by strengthening the commitment of political principals (electorates) to upholding productive property rights.

Other undemocratic institutions can also improve performance through such channels. By removing an insulating layer between political agents and consumer principals, institutions that elect (rather than appoint) regulators can push policy in a pro-consumer direction. In Besley and Stephen Coate's (2003) model, for example, elected regulators choose policies on a single dimension, and electorates retrospectively vote on those choices. Policies from appointed regulators, on the other hand, embed themselves in myriad decisions of corresponding appointers. By increasing the number of dimensions that voters must consider when evaluating regulations, this embedding introduces slack to the agency relationship, letting appointed regulators depart from consumer ideals.[16]

Besley and Coate (2003) thus formalized the hypothesis that having to face (single-dimension) elections strengthens regulators' accountability to consumers (relative to producers), a hypothesis that enjoys considerable empirical support. Guy Holburn and Pablo Spiller (2002) and Besley and Coate (2003), for example, found that consumers face significantly lower electricity rates when public utility commissioners come to office via elections. Susan Smart (1994) developed qualitatively similar evidence for telecommunications service prices.

Besley (2003), Besley and Coate (2003), and Alberto Alesina and Guido Tabellini (2007), in turn, anticipated the potential for lower prices through this channel to retard investment.[17] Electing regulators in these dynamic settings

[16]The literature on mechanism design in "multitasking" environments also highlights "the difficulties of contracting in a multidimensional outcome setting" (Hatfield and Miquel 2006).

[17]Besley and Coate (2003) developed preliminary evidence to this effect.

creates a qualitatively identical implication to what emerged from our static pressure-group model above. In both cases, the "distance" between electoral principals and political agents decreases with electorates' capacity to influence policy. The capital levy problem's dynamics highlight, however, that reducing agency costs increases regulated producers' exposure to re-contracting risk and can thus leave economies resting at inferior outcomes. Starting from a different set of assumptions, a negative relationship between the strength of democratic governance and output again reflects inferior economic performance.

### *1.2.2 What if "Real Options" Are Important?*

Familiar models of both pressure-group competition and dynamic consistency focus on different salient features of many empirical settings (i.e., the potential for regulatory capture and the problem of credible commitment), but agree that a negative relationship between democratic institutions and relevant quantities reflects a weakening of economic performance. This inference appears even more insensitive to assumptions when evaluated in the light of other plausible setups. For example, Ian Dobbs (2004) and Robert Earle et al. (2007) showed that price-capped monopolists can implicitly exercise an option by letting demand uncertainty resolve itself before sinking resources into network development.[18] Consequently, even though commitments are feasible in these dynamic models, producers maintain an increasingly inferior capital stock as price caps become more binding.[19] If, as in Smart (1994), Holburn and Spiller (2002), Besley and Coate (2003), and Falaschetti (2003a), caps tighten with increases in the relative weight that regulators place on consumers' surplus, then the expropriation of "real options" constitutes another channel through which a negative relationship between electoral accountability and equilibrium output can evidence a realized potential for accountability to diminish economic performance.

## 1.3 Conclusion and a Look Ahead

This chapter showed how democratic governance, modeled in various manners, can weaken economic performance. In this light, the "neighborhood of assumptions" on which our investigation is building appears to be "wide", whereas the "corresponding interval of inferences is narrow" (Leamer 1985). Normative conclusions

---

[18]Jerry Hausman (1997) and Hausman and J. Gregory Sidak (1999) argued for the importance of accounting for such options when regulating the price at which incumbent local exchange companies sell unbundled network elements to competitors.

[19]The idea here is that lowering price caps does not change the variance in expected revenues (i.e., price caps do not change uncertainty about the demand curve per se, though they do change where we expect to end up on a given demand curve), but it does reduce the reward for accepting that risk, and thus discourages investment.

from how electoral accountability relates to observable quantities thus exhibit considerable robustness to that relationship's true intermediating channels. Indeed, to the extent that pressure-group competition, dynamic consistency, and real options (each of which finds considerable empirical support in related applications) span the channels through which electoral accountability relates to relevant quantities, reduced form of evidence of that relationship can confidently support conclusions about how democratic governance influences economic performance.

The hypothesis that democratic governance can weaken economic performance appears to logically develop from a rather broad set of reasonable assumptions. Our next question, then, is whether this abstract possibility is empirically important. To address this question, we will need a "natural lab" – an empirical setting where we can control for confounding variables, and thus carefully focus on how institutions that strengthen democratic governance relate to output. In Chapter 2, we will see that the US telecommunications sector offers an attractive setting in this sense. We will examine data from this sector in Chapter 3 and see that output regularly decreases in the presence of institutions that favor consumers over producers (on the margin) – a relationship that our Chapter 1 models agree reflects a realized potential for democratic governance to go too far.

## References

Acemoglu, Daron, Simon Johnson, and James A. Robinson (2001). The colonial origins of comparative development: An empirical investigation. *American Economic Review*, 91(5), 1369–1401.

Alesina, Alberto and Guido Tabellini (2007). Bureaucrats or politicians? Part I: A single policy task. *American Economic Review*, 97(1), 169–179.

Armstrong, Mark and David E. M. Sappington (2006). Regulation, competition, and liberalization. *Journal of Economic Literature* 44(2), 325–366.

Becker, Gary S. (1983). A theory of competition among pressure groups for political influence. *Quarterly Journal of Economics*, 98(3), 371–400.

Bernheim, Douglas B. and Michael D. Whinston (1986). Menu auctions, resource allocation, and economic influence. *Quarterly Journal of Economics*, 101(1), 1–31.

Besley, Timothy (2003). Elected versus appointed regulators. In Charles K. Rowley and Friedrich Schneider (Eds.), *Encyclopedia of Public Choice* (pp. 198–201). New York: Springer.

Besley, Timothy and Robin Burgess (2002). The political economy of government responsiveness: theory and evidence from India. *Quarterly Journal of Economics*, 117(4), 1415–1453.

Besley, Timothy and Stephen Coate (2003). Elected versus appointed regulators: Theory and evidence. *Journal of the European Economic Association*, 1(5), 1176–1206.

Denzau, Arthur T. and Michael C. Munger (1986). Legislators and interest groups: how unorganized interests get represented. *American Political Science Review*, 80(1), 89–106.

Dobbs, Ian (2004). Intertemporal price cap regulation under uncertainty. *Economic Journal*, 114(495), 421–440.

Earle, Robert, Karl Schmedders, and Tymon Tatur (2007). On price caps under uncertainty. *Review of Economic Studies*, 74(1), 93–111.

Falaschetti, Dino (2003a). Can latent groups influence policy decisions? The case of telecommunications policy. *Journal of Law, Economics, and Organization*, 19(1), 83–105.

Falaschetti, Dino (2003b). Credible commitments and investment: Does opportunistic ability or incentive matter? *Economic Inquiry*, 41(4), 660–674.

Fleck, Robert K. (1999). The value of the vote: a model and test of the effects of turnout on distributive policy. *Economic Inquiry*, 37(4), 609–623.

Fleck, Robert K. (2001). Inter-party competition, intra-party competition, and distributive policy: a model and test using new deal data. *Public Choice*, 108(1–2), 77–100.

Garfinkel, Michelle R. and Jaewoo Lee (2000). Political influence and the dynamic consistency of policy. *American Economic Review*, 90(3), 649–666.

Hamilton, James T. (1993). Politics and social costs: estimating the impact of collective action on hazardous waste facilities. *RAND Journal of Economics*, 24(1), 101–125.

Hatfield, John and Gerard Miquel (2006). Multitask Political Agency. Stanford University Graduate School of Business, Working Paper.

Hausman, Jerry A. (1997). Valuation and the effect of regulation on new services in telecommunications. *Brookings Papers on Economic Activity: Microeconomics*, 1–38.

Hausman, Jerry A. and J. Gregory Sidak (1999). A consumer-welfare approach to the mandatory unbundling of telecommunications networks. *Yale Law Journal* 190(3), 417–505.

Hirschman, Albert O. (1970). *Exit, Voice, and Loyalty: Responses to Decline in Firms, Organizations, and States*. Cambridge, MA: Harvard University Press.

Holburn, Guy L. F. and Pablo T. Spiller (2002). Interest Group Representation in Administrative Institutions: The Impact of Consumer Advocates and Elected Commissioners on Regulatory Policy in the United States. University of California Energy Institute (UCEI), Energy Policy and Economics Working Paper.

Key, V. O. Jr. (1984 [1949]). *Southern Politics in State and Nation – A New Edition*. Knoxville, TN: University of Tennessee Press.

Kydland, Finn E. and Edward C. Prescott (1977). Rules rather than discretion: The inconsistency of optimal plans. *Journal of Political Economy*, 85(3),473–491.

Leamer, Edward (1985). Sensitivity analysis would help. *American Economic Review*, 75(3), 308–313.

Levy, Brian and Pablo T. Spiller (1994). The institutional foundations of regulatory commitment: A comparative analysis of telecommunications regulation. *Journal of Law, Economics, and Organization*, 10(2), 201–246.

Lyon, Thomas P. (2003). Capture or contract? The Early Years of Electric Utility Regulation. Indiana University and Resources for the Future, working paper.

Marceau, Nicolas and Michael Smart (2003). Corporate lobbying and commitment failure in capital taxation. *American Economic Review*, 93(1), 241–251.

North, Douglass C. and Barry Weingast (1989). Constitutions and commitment: The evolution of institutions governing public choice in seventeenth century England. *Journal of Economic History*, 49(4), 803–832.

Peltzman, Sam (1976). Toward a more general theory of regulation. *Journal of Law and Economics*, 19(2), 211–240.

Pereira, Joseph (2008a). Price-fixing makes a comeback after Supreme Court ruling. *Wall Street Journal*, August 18, A1.

Pereira, Joseph (2008b). Minimum-price foes to use eBay in effort. *Wall Street Journal*, December 5, B7.

Power to the people (2004). *Wall Street Journal*, March 15, A16.

Rodrik, Dani, Arvind Subramanian, and Francesco Trebbi (2002). Institutions rule: The primacy of institutions over geography and integration in economic development. NBER Working Paper 9305.

Schmalensee, Richard (2004). Sunk costs and antitrust barriers to entry. MIT Sloan School of Management, Working Paper 4457–04 (January).

Sidak, J. Gregory (2001). Mr. Justice Nemo's social statistics. Texas Law Review, 79, 737–765.

Smart, Susan R. (1994). The consequences of appointment methods and party controls for telecommunications pricing. *Journal of Economics and Management Strategy*, 3(2), 301–323.

Stasavage, David (2002). Private investment and political institutions. *Economics and Politics*, 14(1), 41–64.

# Chapter 2
# Natural Experiments

## State Telecom Sectors Offer Attractive Labs for Studying Politics, Law, and Economics

We saw in Chapter 1 that by strengthening the principal–agent relationship between electorates and politicians, democratic governance can protect against collective choices that overly serve concentrated economic interests and thus improve the welfare of consumer electorates while expanding society's economic opportunities more generally. But we also raised the principled concern that electorates can pursue their own concentrated interests, even at the expense of efficiency, and showed that this concern gives rise to a theoretically robust and observable implication – when democratic governance goes too far, firms curb their productive activity and market output decreases as a result.

The US telecommunications sector offers an attractive quasi-experimental setting in which to empirically evaluate this relationship. Importantly, institutions that influence the strength of democratic governance (e.g., campaign finance laws, election and appointment processes, voter registration rules), as well as of corresponding economic activity, vary in a comparable manner across state telecommunication sectors, and the potential for confounding variables to bias statistical inference can be readily addressed. Citing features like these, Timothy Besley and Anne Case (2003) characterized cross-state investigations as being able to yield more confident conclusions about causal relationships than might, say, cross-country studies where unobserved differences between regulatory jurisdictions and hard-to-translate institutional measures can be more difficult to address.

Exploiting this research design's strengths, we will see in Chapter 3 that proxies for stronger democratic institutions (i.e., restrictions on campaign contributions, the selection of regulators through elections (rather than appointments), and voter registration rules that increase turnout) share a statistically significant, economically large, and negative relationship with output. Interpreted within the robust theoretical framework of Chapter 1, this evidence supports the conclusion that democratic governance not only risks giving too much weight to consumer electorates but also has likely weakened economic performance in a sector whose salient features are broadly shared.[1]

[1] Although they may not offer the same quasi-experimental advantages as does the local exchange sector, any sector where institutions expose producers to non-market distributional influences faces

D. Falaschetti, *Democratic Governance and Economic Performance*,
Studies in Public Choice 14, DOI 10.1007/978-0-387-78707-7_2,

In addition, we will see that this evidence is difficult to dismiss as a statistical artifact. For example, to increase confidence that states received a "random treatment" of contribution restrictions, we will employ the innovative method of Joseph Altonji et al. (2005) for gauging "selection on unobservables" when otherwise attractive data lack interesting time series variation or when theory is relatively silent about what constitutes a good instrument.[2] We will also evaluate the theory using alternative proxies for the strength of democratic governance-proxies that, by construction, exhibit considerable independence from confounding variables that might bias inference from measures of campaign finance restrictions. In doing so, we will find that even the lower (absolute) bound of our estimated relationship between democratic governance and economic performance is considerable; that is, an alternative rationalization would have to explain an implausibly large share of this relationship to wholly dismiss it as an artifact.

## 2.1 General Requirements for a Natural Experiment

An attractive setting for estimating the relationship between democratic governance and economic performance would be one where democratic governance randomly varies in its strength, and the response of associated quantities to this variation can readily be observed. The local exchange sector approaches this ideal. Institutions like campaign finance laws, methods for selecting public utility regulators, and rules that govern voter registration exhibit considerable variation across states, and various statistical methods can be used to isolate the portion of this variation that can confidently be treated as random. In addition, the nature of the local exchange technology precludes output from being distributed outside of the jurisdiction in which institutions of interest are located, and the Federal Communications Commission (FCC) reports measures of output that are comparable across those jurisdictions. Features like these make the local exchange sector an attractive laboratory for examining how output responds to plausibly random variation in accountability.

---

this type of risk (e.g., insurance, which we will investigate in Chapter 5). Fred McChesney (1987) carefully anticipated this important possibility.

[2]Altonji, Elder, and Taber's (2005) method appears well-suited to aiding identification in the present application. First, although campaign finance restrictions exhibit considerable cross-state variation, they appear more stable when evaluated within states across time. In addition, the considerable cost of adjusting sunk telecom investments means that our proxy for output (i.e., land-line connections to telecommunications networks) likely exhibits noisy time series variation (e.g., variable lags in responding to stimuli) that can cloud evidence of causal relationships (even if they truly exist). Insight to whether campaign finance restrictions can strengthen economic performance thus appears unlikely to come from the time series dimension of relevant variables. Finally, because our regressors of interest are institutional proxies and theories of endogenous institutions are not very well-developed, good instruments can be difficult to find for the present application.

## 2.2 Experimental Conditions in the Telecommunications Sector

Producing access to telecommunications networks employs an irreversible, capital-intensive technology where local exchange companies (LECs) connect end-users to switching plants via "loops" (e.g., see Hausman and Sidak 1999, Pindyck 2003). A loop generally consists of a pair of twisted copper wires and the portion of associated infrastructure-capacity that these wires consume (e.g., trench and telephone pole space). LECs incur both initial and recurring costs to build and maintain loops and recover some of these costs via connection and line charges (Parsons 1996). If capital employment is sensitive to expectations about this cost recovery, then political forces that influence various regulated prices have a channel through which to exert real economic effects.

While Public Utility Commissions (PUCs) proximately set a number of potentially relevant prices,[3] interested groups in general, and LECs in particular, can exert significant influence.[4] LECs might lobby elected commissioners with contributions that are (perhaps implicitly) contingent on relevant prices. They might also offer contingent support to governors and legislators who, in turn, can influence prices via the appointment process.[5] Finally, whether commissioners are elected or appointed, LECs might influence prices by contingently supporting governors and legislators who, in turn, can sway commissioners by altering a PUC's regulatory authority or budget.[6] These institutional features offer ample opportunity for interested players to "adjust rates in order to achieve political goals" (Brock 1994).

The legal setting in which LECs attempt to influence prices also varies considerably across relevant jurisdictions. For example, the data that we will evaluate in Chapter 3 offer information on 19 (of 48 contiguous) US states where election authorities prohibited contributions from regulated utilities. They also offer information on 23 states that formally restricted contributions, with restriction levels varying from \$25 to \$150,000 per election cycle. By this and other measures, local exchange service producers exhibit considerable variation in their capacity to lobby relevant policy makers.

---

[3]Regulatory jurisdiction over telecommunications policy divides itself between the Federal Communications Commission (FCC) and state public utility or public corporation commissions. States maintain authority over most rates charged to customers for local exchange services. For long-distance services, the FCC regulates interstate service and state regulatory or public utilities commissions regulate intrastate service (Harris and Kraft 1997).

[4]Moreover, because "incumbent" LECs (not "competitive" LECs) tend to maintain sunk investments, they enjoy a comparative advantage in lobbying in models like those of Michelle Garfinkel and Jaewoo Lee (2000) and Nicolas Marceau and Michael Smart (2003).

[5]Nationwide, 12 states elect their public utility commissioners. Others employ an appointment process (Council of State Governments 1999).

[6]Since 1989, several states' legislatures have statutorily constrained utility commissions' authority over telecommunications rates and revenues (Zearfoss 1998). Gerald Brock (1994) argued that such channels for "micromanagement" effectively transform elected legislators into "independent telecommunication policy makers" (independent, that is, of associated regulators).

Finally, the technology for producing local exchange services constrains suppliers from offering services in jurisdictions other than those in which they confront democratic institutions of interest (e.g., lobbying restrictions). The "institutional elasticity" of supply for local exchange carriers is thus likely to be higher than for producers in other networked sectors (e.g., electricity) where output might be transmitted to more favorable regulatory jurisdictions. Likewise, this elasticity may be higher for telecoms than for other producers that also appear sensitive to the capital levy problem. For example, available measures of quantity supplied in high research and development sectors like pharmaceuticals may not strongly respond to our modeled regulatory forces, since that industry's production technology does not constrain output from migrating to markets where those forces are less powerful (efficiency consequences can, nevertheless, remain considerable).

## 2.3 What Should We See if Democratic Governance Goes Too Far in This Application?

While attractive, this quasi-experimental setting leaves open issues that might weaken confidence in the inference that Chapter 3's results make available. Perhaps the most important empirical limit comes from the difficulty of producing evidence on intermediating channels, that is, policies that result from democratically governed public choices and, in turn, influence the quantity of output that firms are willing to supply. For example, our theoretical framework from Chapter 1 suggests that we evaluate a channel like the following:

$$\textit{Campaign Finance Law} \rightarrow \textit{Contributions} \rightarrow \textit{Regulated Price} \rightarrow \textit{Output} \quad (2.1)$$

But considering this channel's first relationship (i.e., *Campaign Finance Law* → *Contributions*) is unlikely to produce insights that are important for our application. Yeon-Koo Che and Ian Gale (1998) showed that by strengthening the incentive for smaller players to enter the game, constraining campaign contributions can reduce, increase, or leave unchanged aggregate contributions.[7] Consequently, even if campaign finance laws truly influence final allocations according to the Chapter 1 theory, an empirical relationship between campaign finance laws and contributions, or contributions and prices, need not exist.

In this light, ignoring intermediating relationships, like that between campaign finance laws and campaign contributions, may not overly weaken our empirical

[7] To see how caps can expand campaign finance activities, consider an all-pay auction where high-valuation players confront a binding cap. By formally reducing feasible bids for "high-valuation" players, such a constraint might be expected to reduce aggregate bidding. But capping high types can also encourage low-valuation players to enter the game. Indeed, absent a constraint, low-valuation players can find their equilibrium probability of winning so low that submitting a bid of "zero" becomes optimal. By encouraging low-valuation players to submit strictly positive bids in equilibrium, caps can thus increase the level of bidding from all players.

research design. The design's cornerstone remains isolating plausibly random variation in the institution of interest (e.g., campaign finance law).

We may still be interested, however, in whether we can safely ignore *Regulated Price* as an intermediating channel. In other words, we may wonder whether the following structure still deserves our attention.

$$\textit{Campaign Finance Law} \rightarrow \textit{Regulated Price} \rightarrow \textit{Output} \tag{2.2}$$

By formally reducing the channel through which democratic institutions can influence economic performance to a single regulated price, our theoretical motivation from Chapter 1 assumes that we can practically make such an evaluation.[8] However, PUCs regulate *numerous* prices, any combination of which might represent the true channel through which lobbying-rules influence real activity in local exchange markets.[9] For example, in addition to pricing the various components of an end-user's services, PUCs can influence the price at which incumbent local exchange carriers (ILECs) must "unbundle" their network components for competitive local exchange carriers (CLECs). But while ILECs frequently cite such pricing (and its interaction with associated retail pricing) as curbing their incentive to invest (e.g., see Jorde et al. 2000, MacAvoy and Sidak 2000, Dreazen and Young 2003, and Pociask 2003), associated regulatory decrees tend to be complex (e.g., see Squeo and Young 2004) and have therefore lacked systematic documentation (e.g., see Abel 2002). Confronted with this complexity, for example, Robert Crandall et al. (2003) excluded from their formal empirical analysis 14 states for which unbundled network element (UNE) prices are not reliable.

Rather than have our inference rely on a price index that has created difficulty with past investigations, we will empirically evaluate the following reduced form of relationship and put our research efforts instead into assessing how confidently the data speak to the *ultimate* effect of democratic institutions on economic performance.

$$\textit{Campaign Finance Law} \rightarrow \textit{Output} \tag{2.3}$$

[8] Rui de Figueiredo and Geoff Edwards (2007) found evidence that, on its face, appears to support this channel – that is, actual contributions influence prices in the hypothesized direction. As modeled in our Chapter 1, however, capital-accumulation decisions ultimately rest on campaign contribution laws (i.e., the *potential* for consumer or producer influence). In addition, de Figueiredo and Edwards gained identification from time series variation in prices. The technology that exposes local exchange carriers to the capital levy problem, however, also creates considerable adjustment costs and thus diminishes the responsiveness of investment to high-frequency price changes.

[9] Contributors (reviewed above) to the public choice literature found a negative relationship between retail price *indexes* and consumers' potential to pressure regulators. If an increase in such pressure decreases an investment-relevant price, then received indexes would have indeed exhibited a negative relationship with electoral accountability. However, such indexes would also be noisy proxies for investigations (like the present one) that focus on how laws influence economic performance (rather than distributions). In this plausible case, measuring variables with error could mask the theoretically robust relationships outlined in Chapter 1, even if those relationships are empirically important.

Considering the reduced-form relationship between output and democratic institutions like campaign finance restrictions arguably addresses the law and economics question of present interest. Identifying relevant channels is important, but perhaps more so for readers who are interested in the telecommunications sector than in the general insights that this research develops about how the political setting in which laws are created ultimately affects economic performance. And while such channels plausibly exist,[10] establishing confidence in any *one* of them encounters considerable difficulty.

## 2.4 Conclusion

A productive research design for our purposes may thus be one that exploits a considerable richness in institutional variation to carefully measure the *gross* relationship between real activity and producers' formal capacity to pressure politicians. To be sure, other literatures have successfully taken such a reduced-form approach. For example, macroeconomists have given theoretical consideration to monetary policy channels while focusing their empirical investigations on what is arguably a more pressing problem-isolating exogenous variation in monetary policy so that causal inference about economic performance can be drawn from non-experimental data.

Finally, a less important (though perhaps not obviously so) limit of working in this sector is one of controlling for unobserved heterogeneity, that is, forces that "truly" influence economic performance but are hard to measure and happen to vary with our institutional proxies. The paucity of time series variation in our proxies for democratic institutions and output, for example, technically discourages us from drawing interesting inference from panel data. While controlling for fixed effects might appear to be attractive for addressing unobserved cross-sectional heterogeneity, doing so in the present application would also cloud inference from coefficient estimates on variables that vary more across space than across time (e.g., campaign finance restrictions).

In addition, while states offer an attractive quasi-experimental setting on several dimensions, they do not always confidently admit an instrumental variable to the present analysis. The popular method of treating lagged endogenous regressors as instruments, for example, runs into difficulties that are both general and particular to our application. When an independent variable of interest (i.e., an indicator of contribution limits) is dichotomous, for example, instrumenting with the initial year of such limits would trivially confirm our OLS results.

More generally, lagged endogenous regressors can be "bad" instruments because, while they can share a strong correlation with the endogenous regressor, they may not be "excludable;" that is, rather than isolating the exogenous variation in a largely

[10] See, for example, Smart (1994), Besley and Coate (2003), and Falaschetti (2003), each of which developed evidence that regulated prices decrease as $\alpha$ increases (i.e., as consumer interests weigh more heavily on regulatory objectives in equation (1.1)).

endogenous regressor, the lagged instrument may correlate with the *same* endogenous variation that biases the OLS estimates. This potential may be especially concerning for cases where endogenous regressors proxy for political institutions. Here, a general theory of how institutions evolve does not appear readily available. But because exclusion restrictions cannot be tested (at least in the just identified case), such a theory is necessary to confidently establish a restriction's validity.[11]

Difficulties like these are common in politics, law, and economics literatures, but stronger substitutes for addressing omitted variables bias (OVB) are becoming available. Altonji et al. (2005), for example, recently developed a method for drawing causal inference from non-experimental data without relying on a priori exclusion restrictions. Coupled with other robustness checks (e.g., employing independent proxies for consumer pressure and examining alternative specifications), Altonji et al.'s method will let us exploit the benefits of working with the present cross-section while carefully addressing difficulties whose mitigation is sometimes thought to require access to panel data or good instruments.

## References

Abel, Jaison R. (2002). Entry into regulated monopoly markets: The development of a competitive fringe in the local telephone industry. *Journal of Law & Economics*, XLV(2, part 1), 289–316.

Altonji, Joseph G., Todd E. Elder, and Christopher R. Taber (2005). Selection on observed variables: Assessing the effectiveness of catholic schools. *Journal of Political Economy*, 113(1), 151–184.

Besley, Timothy and Anne Case (2003). Political institutions and policy choices: Evidence from the United States. *Journal of Economic Literature*, XLI(1), 7–73.

Besley, Timothy and Stephen Coate (2003). Elected versus appointed regulators: Theory and evidence. *Journal of the European Economic Association*, 1(5), 1176–1206.

Brock, Gerald W. (1994). *Telecommunications Policy for the Information Age*. Cambridge and London: Harvard University Press.

Che, Yeon-Koo and Ian Gale (1998). Caps on political lobbying. *American Economic Review*, 88, 643–651.

Council of State Governments (1999). *The Book of the States, 1998–99 Edition, Volume 32*. Lexington, KY: Council of State Governments.

Crandall, Robert W., Allan T. Ingraham, and Hal J. Singer (2003). Do unbundling policies discourage CLEC facilities-based investment? http://ssrn.com/abstract=387421. Accessed 12 March 2003.

[11] To be sure, theory is making progress, but does little to help the present identification problem. Besley and Case (2003) and Thomas Stratmann and Francisco Aparicio-Castillo (2006), for example, used party preference and educational attainment as instruments for campaign finance laws. In our application, however, education can independently relate to equilibrium output through its effect on consumer demand whereas party preference can do so through unobserved policy channels. Channels like these for independent influence can create considerable bias. For example, in unreported 2SLS regressions where measures of education and party preference act as instruments (as opposed to controls), output and consumer pressure continue to share a significant and negative relationship (as they do in corresponding OLS regressions). The coefficient estimates' magnitude, however, is implausibly large.

de Figueiredo, Rui J. P. and Geoff Edwards (2007). Does private money buy public policy? Campaign contributions and regulatory outcomes in telecommunications. *Journal of Economics & Management Strategy*, 16(3), 547–576.

Dreazen, Yochi J. and Shawn Young (2003). FCC plans to erase a key rule aiding local phone competition. *Wall Street Journal*, January 6, A1, A4.

Falaschetti, Dino (2003). Can latent groups influence policy decisions? The case of telecommunications policy. *Journal of Law, Economics, and Organization*, 19(1), 83–105.

Garfinkel, Michelle R. and Jaewoo Lee (2000). Political influence and the dynamic consistency of policy. *American Economic Review*, 90(3), 649–666.

Harris, Robert G. and C. Jeffrey Kraft (1997). Meddling through: Regulating local telephone competition in the United States. *Journal of Economic Perspectives*, 11, 93–112.

Hausman, Jerry A. and J. Gregory Sidak (1999). A consumer-welfare approach to the mandatory unbundling of telecommunications networks. *Yale Law Journal*, 190(3), 417–505.

Jorde, Thomas M., J. Gregory Sidak, and David J. Teece (2000). Innovation, investment and unbundling. *Yale Journal on Regulation*, 17(1), 1–37.

MacAvoy, Paul W. and J. Gregory Sidak (2000). What is wrong with American telecommunications? In J. Gregory Sidak, Christoph Engel, and Guenter Knieps (Eds.) Competition and regulation in telecommunications: Examining Germany and America, (pp. 69–77). Kluwer Academic Publishers.

Marceau, Nicolas and Michael Smart (2003). Corporate lobbying and commitment failure in capital taxation. *American Economic Review*, 93(1), 241–251.

McChesney, Fred S. (1987). Rent extraction and rent creation in the economic theory of regulation. *Journal of Legal Studies*, 16(1), 101–118.

Parsons, Steve G. (1996). The economic necessity of an increased subscriber line charge (SLC) in telecommunications. *Administrative Law Review*, 48, 227–250.

Pindyck, Robert S. (2003). Mandatory unbundling and irreversible investment in telecom networks. MIT Sloan School of Management Working Paper 4452–03 (December).

Pociask, Stephen B. (2003). The effect of bargain wholesale prices on local telephone competition: Does helping competitors help consumers? Sponsored Working Paper, TeleNomic Research, LLC. http://www.telenomic.com. Accessed 2005 March 8.

Smart, Susan R. (1994). The consequences of appointment methods and party controls for telecommunications pricing. *Journal of Economics and Management Strategy*, 3(2), 301–323.

Squeo, Anne Marie and Shawn Young (2004). Court overturns rules governing local telephone competition. *Wall Street Journal*, March 3, A1, A12.

Stratmann, Thomas and Francisco J. Aparicio-Castillo (2006). Competition policy for elections: Do campaign contribution limits matter? *Public Choice*, 127(1–2), 177–206.

Zearfoss, Nancy (1998). The structure of state utility commissions and protection of the captive ratepayer: Is there a connection? National Regulatory Research Institute Working Paper 98–14.

# Chapter 3
# Statistical Evidence

## Democratic Governance Probably Went Too Far in at Least One Important Sector

The title of this book, *Democratic Governance and Economic Performance*, may (at least before the colon) give rise to expectations of confirming our conventional wisdom about democracy. Indeed, as we have documented in previous chapters, popular media and even academic scholarship have characterized democracy as a one-way street to improved social welfare. But our robust theoretical framework from Chapter 1 shows that democracies can become more concerned about electoral distributions than general opportunities. And in the event that democratic governance goes too far in this manner, that chapter also offers formal guidance as to what we should see as evidence of shrinking opportunities.

In this chapter, we will examine data from the "natural laboratory" that the US local exchange sector offers and find persistent evidence that this (up to now) principled concern about democracy going too far is more than a theoretical curiosity. To start, we will see that output in this sector has significantly *decreased* in the presence of constraints on lobbyists' campaign contributions – a popularly regarded democratic institution that is supposed to close the distance between what electoral principals want and what political agents deliver. Moreover, rather than being spurious, this correlation persists through numerous considerations of alternative rationalizations.

The correlation remains strong, for example, even when we statistically give alternative explanations their maximum weight. Normative conclusions from this correlation also hold up across alternative measures of democratic forces, as well as alternative statistical methods for drawing causal inference from non-experimental data. Finally, in none of these instances do proxies for economic performance increase in response to a strengthening of democracy – which would have counted as evidence in support of the hypothesis that democracy (on observed margins) expands economic opportunities. In this light, the possibility that democratic governance not only can weaken but has weakened performance in an important economic sector does not appear negligible.

Even more, this set of empirical results may speak to more than only the efficiency-consequences of democratic governance in the telecommunications sector. In Chapter 2, we argued that this sector is attractive not for its qualitative uniqueness but rather for the relatively controlled setting that it offers; that is, the relative ease with which it lets us approach the experimental conditions that ground

D. Falaschetti, *Democratic Governance and Economic Performance*,
Studies in Public Choice 14, DOI 10.1007/978-0-387-78707-7_3,

our theoretical results from Chapter 1. While this sector is economically important in itself, then, the empirical results that we will develop in the rest of this chapter increase confidence that *whenever* forces associated with pressure group politics, time inconsistency problems, or real options are germane, the risk of democracy going too far is more than a theoretical possibility. This chapter thus concludes Part I of our book not only by offering empirical support for our firmly grounded and logically developed hypothesis from Chapter 1 but also by satisfying our final criterion for a "good theory" (i.e., empirical relevance) and thus equipping us with an analytical framework for evaluating in Part II how democracy, at various levels of governance, affects economic performance.

## 3.1 An Empirical Proxy for Economic Performance

Chapter 1 models imply that measures of output offer a robust proxy for economic performance. Let us start our formal empirical investigation, then, by measuring performance via the variable *Loops*, which equals the number of land-line connections between end-users and switching facilities that incumbent local exchange carriers (ILECs), subject to price-cap regulation, maintained per 1,000 households on 31 December 2000.[1] Table 3.1 summarizes this variable's distribution as well as those for others introduced below.[2]

Recall that each of our Chapter 1 models emphasizes a different dimension of the local exchange sector but agrees that data on accumulated capital (like the variable *Loops*, rather than, say, calling volume) contain information about economic performance. Consider, for example, a pressure group model with an upward sloping supply curve. Here, a negative relationship between consumer-influence and "quantity" evidences a realized potential for consumers to weaken economic performance by creating or enforcing monopsony prices. If the marginal cost of constructing local exchange lines increases (e.g., if costs increase with the distance between marginal customers and local exchange switches), then data on those lines reasonably proxy for "quantity". In this case, it is the physical *possibility* of making a network connection, not the number of connections actually made (e.g., calling volume), that exhibits an increasing marginal cost and thus measures quantity supplied.

If we instead focus on the low marginal cost of producing local exchange services (instead of the increasing marginal cost of constructing lines), *Loops* continues to inform us about economic performance. In this case, models of the capital levy problem become salient and imply that a negative relationship between proxies

[1] These data predate the relaxing of unbundling requirements in 2003, which may have subsequently narrowed the channels through which electoral pressure can influence local exchange quantities. Such channels may still be "policy relevant", however, as consumer groups continue to lobby for the mandatory sharing of broadband lines (e.g., see Crandall and Singer 2007, Wallsten 2007) and the European Commission encourages incumbent operators to grant smaller competitors network access (e.g., see Jolis 2007).

[2] Appendix A describes each variable.

**Table 3.1** Data summary statistics and correlations. Sources for variables: (A) Trends in Telephone Service 2002 – Table 8.2, (B) Feigenbaum and Palmer (2000), (C) Geospatial and Statistical Data Center (GEOSTAT), and (D) Federal Election Commission (2003)

| | Loops | Contribution Limit | Education | Income | Age 65 years | Clinton | Population Density |
|---|---|---|---|---|---|---|---|
| N | 48 | 48 | 48 | 48 | 48 | 48 | 48 |
| Sum | NA | 19 | NA | NA | NA | NA | NA |
| Mean | 1,790.0 | 0.4 | 76.0 | 33,892 | 12.7 | 41.2 | 171.9 |
| Median | 1,734.1 | 0.0 | 76.7 | 32,694 | 12.7 | 42.4 | 79.4 |
| Maximum | 2,795.5 | 1.0 | 85.1 | 49,199 | 18.3 | 53.2 | 1,054.1 |
| Minimum | 963.7 | 0.0 | 64.3 | 24,448 | 8.7 | 24.7 | 4.8 |
| Standard deviation | 369.5 | 0.49 | 5.51 | 5,758 | 1.79 | 5.85 | 239.9 |
| Source | A | B | C | C | C | D | C |

| | Loops | Contribution Limit | Education | Income | Age 65 years | Clinton | Population density |
|---|---|---|---|---|---|---|---|
| Loops | 1.00 | | | | | | |
| Contribution Limit | −0.29 | 1.00 | | | | | |
| Education | 0.30 | −0.19 | 1.00 | | | | |
| Income | 0.63 | −0.08 | 0.45 | 1.00 | | | |
| Age 65 years | −0.39 | 0.18 | −0.17 | −0.14 | 1.00 | | |
| Clinton | 0.02 | −0.03 | −0.42 | 0.22 | 0.15 | 1.00 | |
| Population density | 0.37 | 0.12 | −0.03 | 0.73 | 0.20 | 0.38 | 1.00 |

for consumer-influence (e.g., restrictions on campaign contributions) and accumulated capital (e.g., *Loops*) evidences a realized potential for electoral accountability to become so strong that it encourages democratic governments to opportunistically expropriate sunk investments (e.g., local exchange lines). This channel for weakening economic performance creates no such observable implication for calling volumes.

Finally, "real option" models focus on the value of letting demand uncertainty resolve itself before sinking resources into network connections. By limiting the returns on successful investments, consumer pressure for regulatory unbundling can diminish this option's value (transferring it instead to entering competitors and, ultimately, consumers), thereby increasing the risk of associated returns and discouraging the accumulation of sunk-cost investments (e.g., residential loops). Here, again, a channel exists through which consumer-influence can weaken economic performance, and evidence of that effect appears in the capital with which incumbents supply end-user accessibility, not the intensity with which callers actually exercise a pre-determined capacity for access.

*Loops* also refines a similar dependent variable that Witold Henisz and Bennett Zelner (2001) employed in examining how the policy flexibility of political executives influences the penetration of telecommunications infrastructure. Working with a cross-country dataset, Henisz and Zelner (2001) found a negative relationship between proxies for discretion and penetration, and attributed this relationship to a lack of formal constraints on laggard-governments' "arbitrary behavior".

An increased capacity for such behavior, however, might also coincide with a superior technology for monitoring investment. Regulators whose objective is consumer surplus, for example, face relatively strong incentives to efficiently monitor under "used and useful" rate of return regulation (Gilbert and Newbery 1994). Hence, while the Henisz and Zelner (2001) evidence supports the capital levy interpretation of our theoretical hypothesis, it may also be consistent with a superior outcome where executive-monitoring checks service providers' incentive to overinvest under regulatory distortions.[3]

By drawing on service providers that do not face such distortions (i.e., price-capped ILECs), *Loops* diminishes this alternative interpretation.[4] Indeed, removing the incentive for over-capitalization is one of price-cap (or incentive-) regulation's frequently purported benefits, and the manner in which US regulators have implemented incentive regulation appears to have, in large part, facilitated these benefits' realization (e.g., see Sappington 2002).

Even in repeated games, however, regulators who take consumer surplus as their objective continue to face considerable pressure to act opportunistically under price-cap regulation (Gilbert and Newbery 1994, Levy and Spiller 1994, Spiller 1996). Applied to the telecommunications sector, such actions can be played by re-setting prices "at the end of each price-cap period to eliminate any extra-normal profit", and thus induce relevant firms to "rationally choose not to operate at peak efficiency" (Sappington 2002, p. 285). Paolo Panteghini and Carlo Scarpa (2003)

---

[3]I thank Jonah Gelbach and Roger Noll for highlighting the importance of making this distinction. Harvey Averch and Leland Johnson (1962) offered a seminal treatment of how regulation can distort firms' investment decisions.

[4]Directly addressing this important possibility precludes us, however, from separating residential and business loops. We will thus control in subsequent regressions for the intensity of business usage by holding constant the number of Fortune 500 headquarters and the number of "business access multilines for reporting ILECs as of December 31, 2000" (Federal Communications Commission, 2000, *Statistics of Communications Common Carriers*, Table 2.4). Results from this and other checks are reported in Appendix C and are consistent with the evidence reported in this chapter's main tables. This robustness adds to the confidence from our application of Altonji et al.'s (2005) method (reported below), which implies that selection into "contribution-restricted states" largely occurs on observables. This robustness also suggests that the interesting variation in *Loops* comes from additional residential lines, a suggestion that is furthered in unreported regressions where non-lifeline residential access lines (Federal Communications Commission, 2000, *Statistics of Communications Common Carriers*, Table 2.19) and additional residential lines (Federal Communications Commission, 2002, *Monitoring Report*, Table 1.21) per household are one-quarter to one-third of a standard deviation less in states that restrict campaign finance contributions. Interpreted within the above theoretical framework, these supplementary results evidence an opportunity for LECs to restrict quantities supplied despite universal service commitments. I thank Robert Crandall and a referee at the *Journal of Competition Law and Economics* for highlighting the importance of making this disclosure.

offered illustrative examples where UK regulators, "subject to considerable political pressures", arguably decreased output prices of utilities in just such a manner.

## 3.2 Proxies for Democratic Governance

Our Chapter 1 models also imply that whether democratic governance improves economic performance, on the margin, can be observed in how performance responds to changes in the strength of consumer-electorates' policy influence. To establish our benchmark result, we will measure this influence by whether campaign finance laws restrict interested producers from making campaign contributions, a variable that we will refer to as *Contribution Limit*. We will also check our benchmark's sensitivity to this measure by looking at whether relevant regulators (public utility commissioners, PUCs) are elected or appointed and how easy it is to mobilize voters when policy moves too far from consumer ideals, variables that we will refer to as *Elected PUC* and *Turnout*, respectively.

As a preview to results that we will develop more carefully below, Table 3.2 reports correlations between our proxy for economic performance (*Loops*) and our proxies for democratic governance. Note that this coarse evaluation offers preliminary evidence for the hypothesis that democratic governance can weaken economic performance; that is, each of our governance proxies, *Contribution Limit*, *Elected PUC*, and *Turnout*, shares a negative correlation with our proxy for performance, *Loops*.

**Table 3.2** Correlations between proxy for economic performance (*Loops*) and alternative proxies for democratic governance

| | Loops | Contribution Limit | Elected PUC | Turnout |
|---|---|---|---|---|
| Loops | 1.00 | | | |
| Contribution Limit | −0.29 | 1.00 | | |
| Elected PUC | −0.42 | 0.32 | 1.00 | |
| Turnout | −0.36 | 0.07 | −0.12 | 1.00 |

The remainder of this section describes each of these variables more completely. The next section, then, develops evidence that rather than being spurious, these correlations exhibit considerable robustness to alternative explanations.

### *3.2.1 Restrictions on Campaign Contributions*

Campaign finance restrictions continually attract political, legal, and scholarly attention as a mechanism for making political agents more accountable to their electoral principals; that is, for their potential to strengthen democratic governance. Anthony Corrado (2000) has argued, for example, that Congress repeatedly fails to tighten these restrictions, even though the public continually ranks the issue as a high priority. Robert Greenberger (2003) made a similar observation, echoing popular arguments like "too much money is spent", "smaller contributions are better than larger ones", "money buys elections", and "money corrupts politicians" (Corrado et al. 1997, p. 96).[5] More forcefully, *Common Cause* president Chellie Pingree characterized contributions as the "*toxic link* between donors who write six-figure checks and people in power."[6]

In this light, restricting campaign contributions appears to be a dominant strategy. Recall, however, that Chapter 1 models highlight how such reforms can work for *or* against economic performance. Restricting contributions, for example, can increase an economy's total product by checking producer monopolies, but can also reduce output by accommodating consumer monopsonies, weakening regulatory commitments, or diminishing the value of real options.

Evidence that these latter implications are more than theoretical curiosities appears in the present chapter's dataset. As noted in the introduction to this section, our baseline measure of democratic pressures will be the independent variable, *Contribution Limit*, which equals one for states that prohibited regulated utilities from contributing to campaigns in 2000. Notice that, if electoral accountability increases with *Contribution Limit*, then our pressure group and other relevant models from Chapter 1 imply that *Loops* should increase (holding other considerations constant) with *Contribution Limit* in applications where democratic governance improves economic performance. But as Table 3.2 summarizes, a coarse evaluation of these variables produces preliminary evidence *against* the hypothesis that democratic governance necessarily strengthens performance. Here, *Loops* and *Contribution Limit* share a considerable and negative correlation (i.e., −0.29), and as our more rigorous evaluation shows below, this correlation stands up to the possibility of alternative explanations.

## 3.2.2 Alternative Measures of Democratic Governance

To be sure, an immediate and legitimate concern about this type of evaluation is that correlation does not imply causation. One of the robustness checks that we will formally develop in this chapter's remainder, then, will be an evaluation of how *Loops* relates to other measures of democratic governance – importantly, measures that reasonably vary with the strength of democratic governance but maintain some independence from the variable *Contribution Limit*. The idea here is that if *Contribution Limit* and the alternative measures each contain information about the

---

[5] Michael Bailey (2004) further documented this conventional wisdom.

[6] *Common Cause* is a prominent, nonpartisan, citizens' lobbying group. Pingree is quoted (italics added here) in the article "Supreme court decision upholding soft money ban is major victory for America." http://www.commoncause.org/news/default.cfm?ArtID=258. Accessed 16 March 2004.

strength of democratic governance, then they should all exhibit the type of negative correlation that we saw above. Even more, to the extent that these alternatives vary independently from *Contribution Limit*, we can gain confidence that our preliminary negative correlation between *Contribution Limit* and *Loops* reflects forces associated with democratic governance per se, rather than an unrelated variable that is spuriously correlated with our proxy for democratic governance. The correlations reported in Table 3.2 stand up to considerations like these as well as to more rigorous statistical analysis that we will develop in the following section.

#### 3.2.2.1 Elected vs. Appointed Regulators

By removing a layer of insulation between political agents and consumer principals, institutions that elect (rather than appoint) regulators can push policy in a pro-consumer direction. Timothy Besley and Stephen Coate (2003) developed a model, for example, where elected regulators choose policies on a single dimension, and electorates retrospectively vote on those choices. Policies from appointed regulators, on the other hand, embed themselves in myriad decisions of corresponding appointers. By increasing the number of dimensions that voters must consider when evaluating regulations, this embedding introduces slack to the agency relationship, letting appointed regulators more easily depart from consumer ideals.[7]

Besley and Coate (2003) thus formalized the hypothesis that having to face low dimensional elections strengthens regulators' accountability to consumers, a hypothesis that enjoys considerable empirical support. Guy Holburn and Pablo Spiller (2002) and Besley and Coate (2003), for example, found that consumers face significantly lower electricity rates when PUCs come to office via elections. Susan Smart (1994) developed qualitatively similar evidence for telecommunications service prices.

Pushing this public choice insight in a normative direction, Alberto Alesina and Guido Tabellini (2007) showed that appointing bureaucrats (rather than electing politicians) can improve economic performance, especially when commitment problems are salient (as they are in our telecommunications application).[8] As an alternative measure of democratic governance, then, we will employ the variable *Elected PUC*, which equals one for states that elected (rather than appointed) their PUCs as of 1996.[9] And as Table 3.2 reports, this alternative also shares a substantial and

[7]The literature on mechanism design in "multitasking" environments also highlights "the difficulties of contracting in a multidimensional outcome setting" (Hatfield and Miquel 2006).

[8]Recall from our Chapter 1 models that the technology for producing local exchange services exposes carriers to a capital levy problem. Jerry Hausman (1997) and Robert Pindyck (2003), among others, have previously made this observation.

[9]The set of elected states includes Alabama, Arizona, Georgia, Louisiana, Mississippi, Montana, Nebraska, North Dakota, Oklahoma, South Carolina, South Dakota, and Tennessee (Council of State Governments *The Book of the States* 1999, Table 7.43). This variable plays a central role in Falaschetti's (2007) evaluation of how democratic governance influences economic performance.

negative correlation with *Loops* (i.e., $\rho = -0.42$), consistent again with democratic governance weakening economic performance.

#### 3.2.2.2 Voter Turnout

Chapter 2 of this book argues that cross-state institutional variation contributes to the attractiveness of the local exchange sector as a lab for examining how democratic governance influences economic performance. Exploiting this general property, Roger Noll (1986) identified a particular channel through which state-specific political forces can influence the investment incentives of local exchange companies. In particular, Noll anticipated Douglas Arnold's (1991) insight about how the *potential* to mobilize electorates influences policy, arguing that

> To the extent that the basic exchange rate becomes a salient political issue at the state and local level, incumbent legislators could become vulnerable to challenges based in part on their association with the big increases in telephone prices.

That political agents can reasonably expect this issue to become salient is evident in Representative Timothy Wirth's (D, CO) early 1980s election fortunes.[10] While telecommunications policy can be complex, residential users can easily monitor its effects on associated prices. Consequently, potential challengers have a pliable and transparent policy with which to mobilize otherwise "inattentive publics". Challengers may have employed this issue against Wirth, a prominent advocate of telecommunications deregulation. Indeed, when deregulation increased local exchange prices, Wirth's winning margin slipped by almost 10%. Wirth's principal assistant attributed this drop to the price increase (Arnold 1991).

Other informal evidence also appears consistent with political agents being sensitive to residential users' preferences over local service policy. For example, as part of the telephone industry deregulation and breakup of AT&T, the Federal Communications Commission (FCC) attempted to increase a component of residential users' access fee by $6 per month. The House, however, voted overwhelmingly to bar this increase's implementation. The proposed increase

> was a visible, immediate addition to every customer's telephone bill... It was thus relatively easy to create a 'consumer rip-off' issue alleging that this was a plan to help large businesses... at the expense of ordinary consumers (Brock 1994).

The Senate was about to concur with the House when the FCC postponed the increase. Subsequently, the FCC implemented a $1.00 fee with increases phased in annually (Arnold 1991).[11]

[10] More recent evidence that such expectations are reasonable comes from the close political attention to the sensitivity of retail phone bills to how local exchange networks are unbundled (e.g., see Squeo 2004).

[11] Note that this example illustrates how political risks that are relevant for local exchange investment decisions may share a weak correlation with relevant prices and that regulatory authorities can proximately influence a number of prices.

The common motivation for these anecdotes is the hypothesis that politicians weigh consumer preferences against producer interests by considering the likelihood that electorates will mobilize when policies on which they agree (e.g., end-user telecommunications prices) move against them. Falaschetti (2003) supported this hypothesis with evidence that aggregated local exchange prices and electoral mobility share a significant and negative relationship. In this light, whether PUCs receive pressure directly from electoral constituencies or indirectly via federal and state legislators and executives, channels appear to exist through which mobility can weigh on telecommunications prices. If, in turn, these prices influence LECs' asset returns, then associated output should vary accordingly and offer empirical insight to mobility's influence on economic performance.

Given this motivation for how the potential to mobilize electorates can influence policy before the fact, we will employ the variable *Turnout* as an additional proxy for the strength of democratic governance. *Turnout* equals the average percentage of voting age individuals who cast ballots for the office of president in the 1992, 1996, and 2000 general elections,[12] and as reported in Table 3.2, also shares a substantial and negative correlation with *Loops* (i.e., $\rho = -0.36$).

## 3.3 From Correlation to Evidence of Causation

### 3.3.1 Holding Supply and Demand Conditions Constant

Table 3.2 reports several negative correlations between proxies for democratic governance and economic performance, consistent with a realized potential for electoral accountability to go too far. To more carefully evaluate whether these correlations evidence a causal relationship, we can control for alternative explanations that our simple correlation analysis cannot consider. In particular, let us start by estimating parameters from the following model:

$$Loops_i = \beta \cdot Contribution\ Limit_i + \sum_{k=1}^{K} \gamma_k \cdot Controls_{k,i} + u_i \tag{3.1}$$

[12]Averaging voter turnout over several years reduces the error in measuring each constituency's *capacity* to produce political support. Because our investigation is restricted to cross-sectional data, employing any particular year's turnout would increase exposure to potentially spurious year-specific shocks. Nevertheless, our results do not appear (in unreported regressions) sensitive to employing any particular years' turnout as a regressor. In addition, they do not appear sensitive either to employing a longer run average (i.e., from 1960 through 2000) of turnout or to instrumenting for the potentially endogenouts regressor (i.e., *Turnout*) as explained more fully below. *Turnout*'s mean is 54.69 with a standard deviation of 6.52 (Federal Election Commission). This variable plays a central role in Falaschetti's (2005) evaluation of how democratic governance influences economic performance.

**Table 3.3** Ordinary least squares (OLS) coefficient estimates of a proxy for democratic governance (*Contribution Limit*) and controls on a proxy for economic performance (the dependent variable, *Loops*). Standard errors are White heteroskedasticity-consistent

| Variable | (1) Coefficient | SE | (2) Coefficient | SE | (3) Coefficient | SE |
|---|---|---|---|---|---|---|
| Constant | 1,877.18 | 64.81*** | 2,414.91 | 736.63*** | 2,179.41 | 721.06*** |
| Contribution Limit | −220.28 | 106.53** | −174.55 | 89.43* | −147.92 | 85.08* |
| Interaction Term | | | | | 0.09 | 0.05* |
| Education | | | −12.38 | 10.59 | −7.40 | 10.52 |
| Income | | | 44.78 | 13.36 | 37.55 | 13.14*** |
| Age 65 years | | | −51.88 | 37.36*** | −36.78 | 42.53 |
| Clinton | | | −11.52 | 8.71 | −13.79 | 10.09 |
| Population Density | | | 0.00 | 0.26 | 0.09 | 0.23 |
| $N$ | 48 | | 48 | | 43 | |
| $R^2$ | 0.09 | | 0.55 | | 0.55 | |
| Adjusted $R^2$ | 0.07 | | 0.48 | | 0.46 | |
| $\bar{y}$ | 1,789.98 | | 1,789.98 | | 1,788.73 | |
| $\sigma_y$ | 369.45 | | 369.45 | | 374.56 | |
| $F$-statistics | 4.37 | | 8.26 | | 6.13 | |
| Probability ($F$-statistics) | 0.04 | | 0.00 | | 0.00 | |

***, **, and * respectively indicate confidence at the 99%, 95%, and 90% levels

Results from this estimation, a representative sample of which appears in Table 3.3, continue to be consistent with a realized potential for contribution limits to facilitate consumer monopsonies, weaken regulatory commitments, or ease the expropriation of real options.

Regression (1) let us draw more precise inference about the correlation between *Contribution Limit* and *Loops* (recall that Table 3.2 reports this correlation as –0.29). In this very simple specification, the coefficient estimate on *Contribution Limit* (–220.28) says that LECs in states that permit contributions from regulated industries supply over one-half a standard deviation more local exchange services (as measured by *Loops*) than do LECs in states that prohibit contributions. Even more than being statistically significant, then, this preliminary estimate is consistent with an economically large effect.

To gain confidence that this relationship evidences a *causal* relationship, we can rigorously evaluate the potential for heretofore omitted variables to offer an alternative rationalization. In regression (2), we begin this evaluation by following the advice of the theoretical motivation of Chapter 1 to control for 'tastes and technology' - the fundamental forces behind our supply and demand analysis. We can control for consumers' budget constraints and preferences (both economic and political), for example, by employing the variables *Education*, *Income*, *Age 65*, and

*Clinton.*[13] And to address supply-side forces, we can control for the costs that local exchange carriers incur for maintaining loops via the regressor *Population Density.*[14]

The magnitude of the coefficient estimate on *Contribution Limit* (i.e., –174.55), however, does not appreciably decrease. Indeed, the estimate from this specification is consistent with "contribution-prohibited" LECs supplying almost one-half a standard deviation less services than do LECs in states that formally permit campaign contributions.

In regression (3), we consider a finer measure of campaign finance laws by distinguishing between states that (i) *prohibit* contributions from regulated sectors, (ii) *restrict* contributions, and (iii) *do not restrict* contributions. In particular, we let *Contribution Limit* equal one in this specification for states that either prohibit or restrict contributions and introduce an *Interaction Term* (i.e., *Contribution Limit* multiplied by the lowest level at which states formally cap relevant contributions) to facilitate inference on how output reacts to relaxing campaign finance constraints. The results corroborate those from our discrete measure of campaign finance laws, for example, "contribution-prohibited" LECs continue to supply almost one-half a standard deviation less services than do those who can make contributions, while LECs operating in a more relaxed setting (i.e., states that permit an "average" level of contributions, or about $580) supply approximately one-quarter of a standard deviation less services.[15]

## *3.3.2 Subtracting Even the Maximum Bias from Our Coefficient Estimate Leaves a Large Result*

Interpreted within salient models of pressure groups, capital levies, or real options, these results so far weigh against the popular characterization that democratic institutions, like campaign finance restrictions, necessarily strengthen economic performance. Instead, they offer preliminary empirical support for the hypothesis that restrictions can retard performance by facilitating consumers' monopsonistic ambitions, weakening regulatory commitments, or easing the expropriation of real options.

The fact that the negative correlation between *Loops* and *Contribution Limit* (see Table 3.2) continues to appear substantive when we add a firmly grounded set of covariates to our regression specifications, and consider an alternative proxy for campaign finance constraints (see Table 3.3), begins to offer confidence that

[13] Table 3.1 describes these variables.

[14] U. Sankar (1972, equation 10) and Jaison Abel (2002) formally developed similar specifications for related applications.

[15] A lack of data on restriction *levels* does not allow for a full set of observations for this part of our examination. Limiting the dataset in regressions (1) and (2) to only those observations for which restriction levels are observable, however, does not change reported inferences.

this relationship is not a statistical artifact. To further evaluate this robustness, we can apply the innovative method of Joseph Altonji et al. (2005) for considering whether variables that we have still not considered (unobservables) can alternatively rationalize our estimated relationship between proxies for democratic governance and economic performance. This method cleverly exploits information about how our control variables (observables) might have helped self-select states into the "contribution limit treatment group" to estimate the *maximum* bias that unobservables could have created for our coefficient estimates. Using this method, we can thus formally consider whether even the strongest alternative hypothesis would render the relationship between *Contribution Limit* and *Loops* negligible.

This consideration builds from a comparison of the following two normalized index-shifts:

$$\frac{E\left[u|Contribution\ Limit = 0\right] - E\left[u|Contribution\ Limit = 1\right]}{Var\left[u\right]} \tag{3.2}$$

and

$$\frac{E\left[X'\gamma|Contribution\ Limit = 0\right] - E\left[X'\gamma|Contribution\ Limit = 1\right]}{Var\left[X'\gamma\right]} \tag{3.3}$$

where $X'\gamma$ is a series of fitted values that predicts *Loops* (without information about *Contribution Limit*) and $u$ is a series of associated residuals.[16] In short, indexes (3.2) and (3.3) measure the degrees to which relevant variation in unobservables and observables, respectively, intersect the relationship that interests us between campaign finance laws and local exchange loops in the reduced form model (3.1).

To the extent that our observed regressors have fully accounted for non-random selection into "contribution-prohibited" states, the normalized shift of unobservables (3.2) equals zero, and omitted variables cannot have biased the inference that specification (2) from Table 3.3 makes available. But how strongly can we rely on our regressions being *perfectly* specified in this regard?

To evaluate the extent to which inference rests on such strong assumptions, Altonji et al. (2005) showed that selection on observables can proxy for the *maximum* selection on unobservables, and thus developed a bound on how much of the OLS estimate can be attributed to endogeneity bias. Note that if our regressions are randomly specified (as opposed to perfectly specified, which is necessary for an unbiased OLS estimate), then the normalized shift in unobservables (index 3.2) equals that in observables (index 3.3). Under this *worst-case* assumption, readily available information about selection on observables contains otherwise

[16]Interpreted within equation (3.1), $X_i'\gamma = \sum \gamma_k \cdot Controls_{k,i}$. In what follows, we thus refer to a specification where $X$ contains all of the independent variables of regression (2) (except *Contribution Limit*). This relatively sparse specification maintains the *greatest* (non-trivial) potential of those reported in Table 3.3 to evidence bias if omitted variables are truly influential.

unavailable information about selection on unobservables.[17] Altonji et al. (2005) exploited this assumption to estimate the *maximum* selection on unobservables, which, applied to our case,[18] implies a "lower absolute bound" on *Contribution Limit*'s coefficient of –124.80; that is, *Loops* decreases by at least 1/3 of a standard deviation when moving from states that allow contributions to those that prohibit contributions.[19]

Even this lower bound exhibits a considerable magnitude. In addition, it persists across evaluations that test the applied integrity of Altonji et al.'s (2005) method. To be sure, note that if this method is valid, then coefficient estimates on *Contribution Limit* should appear stable when we expand the set of covariates that appear in regression (2) of Table 3.3 (Gelbach 2004, Altonji et al. 2005). A representative set of results reported in Table 3.4 offers confidence in this regard.[20]

Consistent with this stability-implication from Altonji et al.'s (2005) method, inference that can be drawn from these coefficient estimates on *Contribution Limit* exhibits considerable robustness to how we specified relevant regressions. Regression (4) controls, for example, for an expanded set of demographic characteristics (i.e., measures of total population and the percentages of population that are black and white). In doing so, it further addresses *Contribution Limit*'s potential to proxy for "congealed preferences" (rather than relative political pressure from electoral principals) (Riker 1980). Regressions (5) and (6) then add a set of indicators that, respectively, control for regional (i.e., South and West) and firm-level (i.e., ILEC)

---

[17]Inference from Altonji et al.'s (2005) method does not *require* regressions to be randomly specified. Rather, it assumes a random specification to bound the OLS estimate's bias. This assumption, like that for an unbiased OLS estimate, is strong. The "true" coefficient, therefore, likely lies between the OLS estimate and the lower (absolute) bound from the Altonji et al.'s method. To the extent that this interval contains economically large coefficient values, confidence can be gained that the econometric estimate under consideration is not a statistical artifact.

[18]Appendix B reports detailed data from which the shift indexes can be estimated.

[19]The corresponding upper (absolute) bound can be calculated by assuming that selection occurs only on observables, and thus equals the OLS estimate (Altonji et al. 2005).

[20]Other robustness checks include an evaluation of whether the coefficient estimate on *Contribution Limit* is an artifact of influential observations. For example, we can delete from the dataset those observations that most influence the regression line's slope (i.e., the three largest positive- and negative-residual observations from regression (2) (see Table 3.3), which are Arizona, Florida, Nevada, North Dakota, Ohio, and South Carolina). As can be expected, deleting such outliers increases explanatory power (as measured by $R^2$). But, as evidenced in Appendix C (see regression (C)), this increase comes from residual variation in *Loops* that is unrelated to *Contribution Limit*. Treating this issue more generally, we can randomly choose states (with replacement) to construct a new set of observations, estimate the coefficient on *Contribution Limit* (using the specification from regression (2)), and repeat this process 1,000 times. Because each of these 1,000 datasets randomly excludes observations, any sensitivity of the coefficient estimate to particular states should cause these "bootstrapped" estimates to differ from those reported in our main tables. The mean of the bootstrapped estimates (i.e., –290.5), however, exhibits the same magnitude as those reported above and, also like estimates reported above, the 90% confidence interval of [–555.5, –26.0] does not include zero. Appendix C details the frequency distribution of these coefficient estimates.

effects. In doing so, they attempt to hold constant potentially relevant, but heretofore unobserved, cross-sectional heterogeneity (e.g., the capacity for campaign finance institutions to reflect associated LECs' attributes). In each case, however, the coefficient estimate on *Contribution Limit* remains negative and statistically significant, while maintaining the same magnitude of its counterpart in the more parsimonious specification of regression (2) (i.e., –174.55).

### 3.3.3 Results from Synthetic Experiments Add Even More Confidence That Accountability Went Too Far

So far, we have considered the robustness of our application of Altonji et al.'s (2005) method by considering the stability of our OLS coefficient estimate on *Contribution Limit* (regression (2) reported in Table 3.3) to the addition of potentially influential (but previously omitted) explanatory variables. To push this consideration even further, we can introduce new proxies for democratic governance and apply alternative methods for checking whether their relationship with *Loops* evidences causality or instead reflects a spurious correlation.

Returning to Table 3.4, the specification of regression (7) builds on evidence from Smart (1994) and Besley and Coate (2003) that the capacity for regulated utilities to pressure PUCs is relatively small in states that elect their utility commissioners.[21] Here, we employ the indicator *Elected PUC* as an alternative proxy for the relative pressure that electoral principals can exert on regulators. Regression (8), in turn, builds on evidence from Arnold (1991) and Falaschetti (2003) that producers' relative pressure decreases with increased electoral mobility. Here, we employ the variable *Turnout* as another proxy for democratic governance. In both cases, the negative and significant relationships between *Loops* and alternative proxies for democratic governance support the same inference as does our estimated relationship between *Loops* and *Contribution Limit* - local exchange sectors rest at significantly smaller quantities (both statistically and economically) in states where producer pressure is relatively weak.

Results from regression (9) further our confidence that the estimated relationship between *Loops* and *Contribution Limit* is not a statistical artifact. In this specification, the coefficient estimates on *Contribution Limit* and *Elected PUC* remain negative but become statistically insignificant. They jointly remain significant, however, which can be expected if a weakening of producer pressure truly associates itself with a decrease in quantities, but the regressors that measure this relative weakness are collinear. Consistent with this condition, *Contribution Limit* and

[21] Besley and Coate (2003) developed evidence that electoral constituencies recognized significantly lower electricity prices in US states that elect (rather than appoint) relevant regulators. Smart (1994) developed analogous evidence for the telecommunications sector. To the extent that consumer monopsonies or regulatory commitments are empirically relevant, extending this evidence to the present research suggests that telecommunications capital stocks should be relatively low, holding other considerations constant, in states that elect their PUC members.

**Table 3.4** Ordinary least squares (OLS) coefficient estimates of a proxy for democratic governance (*Contribution Limit*) and controls on a proxy for economic performance (the dependent variable, *Loops*). Standard errors are White heteroskedasticity-consistent

| Variable | (4) Coefficient | SE | (5) Coefficient | SE | (6) Coefficient | SE |
|---|---|---|---|---|---|---|
| Constant | 2,458.39 | 1,058.05** | 1,890.13 | 1,188.02 | 1,632.57 | 1,355.49 |
| Contribution Limit | −165.22 | 90.84* | −148.22 | 82.26* | −145.39 | 77.33* |
| Education | −11.19 | 14.48 | −18.26 | 14.23 | 0.14 | 16.62 |
| Income | 40.58 | 17.93** | 58.27 | 17.34*** | 37.33 | 13.80*** |
| Age 65 | −53.20 | 42.38 | −33.39 | 40.69 | −63.14 | 31.62** |
| Clinton | −11.76 | 8.51 | −7.18 | 8.10 | −8.98 | 8.25 |
| Population Density | 0.07 | 0.31 | −0.09 | 0.28 | 0.19 | 0.28 |
| Congealed Prefs? | Yes | | No | | No | |
| Region Effects? | No | | Yes | | No | |
| Firm Effects? | No | | No | | Yes | |
| N | 48 | | 48 | | 48 | |
| $R^2$ | 0.56 | | 0.59 | | 0.63 | |
| Adjusted $R^2$ | 0.45 | | 0.50 | | 0.51 | |
| $\bar{y}$ | 1,789.98 | | 1,789.98 | | 1,789.98 | |
| $\sigma_y$ | 369.45 | | 369.45 | | 369.45 | |
| $F$-statistics | 5.31 | | 6.96 | | 5.48 | |
| Probability ($F$-statistics) | 0.00 | | 0.00 | | 0.00 | |

| Variable | (7) Coefficient | SE | (8) Coefficient | SE | (9) Coefficient | SE |
|---|---|---|---|---|---|---|
| Constant | 2,838.34 | 736.65*** | 997.84 | 705.04 | 1,826.57 | 706.64*** |
| Contribution Limit | | | | | −69.85 | 70.61 |
| Elected PUC | −197.92 | 120.93* | | | −147.69 | 90.87 |
| Turnout | | | −35.89 | 8.82*** | −33.69 | 8.94*** |
| Education | −14.29 | 10.66 | 28.90 | 9.72*** | 21.60 | 10.90** |
| Income | 41.43 | 15.17*** | 28.71 | 9.61*** | 25.49 | 9.46*** |
| Age 65 | −58.78 | 38.68 | −26.57 | 31.88 | −27.10 | 28.69 |
| Clinton | −13.64 | 8.29 | −2.14 | 7.01 | −7.53 | 7.00 |
| Population Density | −0.06 | 0.28 | 0.06 | 0.19 | 0.11 | 0.20 |
| N | 48 | | 48 | | 48 | |
| $R^2$ | 0.54 | | 0.70 | | 0.74 | |
| Adjusted $R^2$ | 0.47 | | 0.66 | | 0.68 | |
| $\bar{y}$ | 1,789.98 | | 1,789.98 | | 1,789.98 | |
| $\sigma_y$ | 369.45 | | 369.45 | | 369.45 | |
| $F$-statistics | 7.88 | | 16.10 | | 13.66 | |
| Probability ($F$-statistics) | 0.00 | | 0.00 | | 0.00 | |

***, **, and * respectively indicate confidence at the 99%, 95%, and 90% levels

*Elected PUC* exhibit considerable collinearity (e.g., $\rho_{\textit{Contribution Limit, Elected PUC}} = 0.32$). The coefficient estimate on *Turnout*, on the other hand, remains negative and retains its significance. This result is similarly expected if the regressors that measure this relative weakness are instead largely independent. Consistent with this condition, *Contribution Limit* and *Turnout* exhibit considerably less collinearity (e.g., $\rho_{\textit{Contribution Limit, Turnout}} = 0.07$).

#### 3.3.3.1 Instrumental Variable Results on Elected Versus Appointed Regulators

As a final "natural experiment" strategy, we can attempt to "instrument" for our alternative proxies for democratic governance-*Elected PUC* and *Turnout*. The idea for an instrument is to find a variable that affects the outcome of interest (e.g., *Loops*) *only* through its relationship with the potentially endogenous variable of interest (e.g., *Elected PUC* or *Turnout*). Notice that if an instrument is successful in this regard, then the instrumental variable estimate of how the independent and dependent variables relate cannot logically be dismissed as an artifact of an alternative rationalization.

A famous application nicely illustrates this method.[22] Angrist and Krueger (2001) used the quarter in which an individual was born to instrument for the years of schooling that he or she received. The goal here was to estimate the economic returns to schooling, and the complication was that individuals with greater inherent skill, motivation, family connections, etc., may have self-selected into more years of schooling and thus created a spurious correlation between schooling and earnings. The quarter of birth, however, is plausibly unrelated to these unobserved variables but still influences the number of schooling years through its relationship with compulsory schooling laws. By isolating this exogenous variation in years of schooling, the quarter of birth instrument could thus facilitate a less-biased estimate of how schooling causally relates to earnings.

To further check whether the large and negative OLS coefficient estimate on *Elected PUC* (reported in Table 3.4) reflects a statistical artifact, or instead evidences a realized potential for democratic governance to weaken economic performance, we might thus re-estimate that coefficient using an instrumental variable. The endogenous institutions' literature following Torsten Persson and Lars Svensson (1989), Alesina and Tabellini (1990), and Andrew Hanssen (2004) offers guidance, suggesting that a measure of political competition might provide a good instrument. These authors started with the assumption that incumbent politicians maintain preferences over not only current policies, but also those that prevail after they leave office. Noting that increases in the competitiveness of elections increases the probability that incumbents will leave office, they then showed that politicians who

[22]Joshua Angrist and Alan Krueger (1991) developed an accessible and authoritative introduction to this quantitative method.

confront the prospect of competitive elections face a relatively strong incentive to insulate current policies from the pressures of future politicians.

Given this theoretical motivation, Falaschetti (2005) argued that the measure of political competition of Steven Levitt and James Poterba (1999) can be a good instrument for *Elected PUC*. For each sampled state, this instrument equals the average (1952–1990) negative absolute difference (in percents) between votes for the Democratic presidential candidate and the national average for that candidate. Levitt and Poterba (1999) interpreted states with vote outcomes equal to (far from) the national average as being "highly" (not very) competitive.

Fig. 3.1 illustrates the distribution of the instrumental variable coefficient estimate on *Elected PUC* from applying the "unbiased split-sample" method to the present case.[23] This estimation method checks the instrumental variable estimator's potential for bias in finite samples[24] by breaking the channel through which "structural" (i.e., second stage) and "reduced form" (i.e., first stage) residuals can be correlated.[25] Inference from this calculation can then be made available by

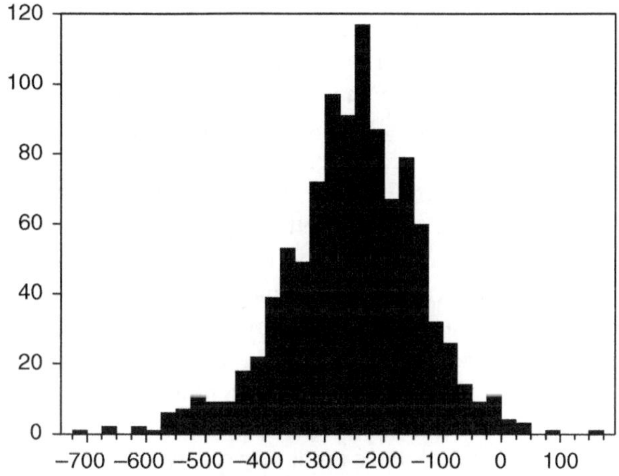


| | |
|---|---|
| Re-Samples | 1,000 |
| Mean | −254.5 |
| Standard Deviation | 112.1 |
| Upper-Bound 90% Confidence Interval | −78.25 |
| Lower-Bound 90% Confidence Interval | −447.3 |
| Maximum | 173.8 |
| Minimum | −718.5 |

**Fig. 3.1** Bootstrapped distribution of the USSIV coefficient estimate on *Elected PUC*

[23]Falaschetti (2005) reported a more complete set of results.

[24]See, for example, Angrist and Krueger (1995) and Hahn and Hausman (2002).

[25]This break comes from estimating one sub-sample's optimal instrument from the other's reduced form parameter estimates. For bias to persist, errors from one sub-sample's reduced form have to be correlated with those from the other's structural equation. Angrist and Krueger (1995) carefully developed this estimator.

"re-sampling" the USSIV estimation procedure, the result of which is summarized in Fig. 3.1.

The large and negative coefficient estimate on *Elected PUC* persists across this robustness check as well. The bootstrapped distribution's mean (i.e., –254.5) implies that the bias-corrected estimate of *Elected PUC*'s coefficient is slightly larger than its OLS counterpart from a similar specification in Table 3.4's column (7) (i.e., – 197.92). In addition, despite the USSIV estimator's inefficiency, inference that is available from the associated confidence intervals continues to support the proposition that a negative relationship between *Loops* and *Elected PUC* reflects the capacity for electoral accountability to significantly reduce total surplus. Indeed, the hypothesis that the bootstrapped distribution's mean equals zero can be rejected at any reasonable level of confidence ($t$-statistic = –71.8).

#### 3.3.3.2 Instrumental Variable Results on Voter Turnout

A similar identification strategy can be used to evaluate the robustness of our Table 3.4 coefficient estimate on *Turnout* to alternative explanations. Here, we can employ the variable *Election Day Registration* (*EDR*) as an instrument.[26] For inference from the resulting coefficient estimate to be valid, *EDR* must share a strong first stage or "reduced form" relationship with *Turnout* (i.e., the potentially endogenous regressor), but maintain no independent variation with *Loops* (i.e., it must be redundant in the second stage or "structural" equation). Evidence appearing in the voter turnout literature suggests that *EDR* is a good instrument, at least with respect to this first criterion. For example, following Wolfinger and Rosenstone's (1980) seminal work, Samuel Patterson and Gregory Caldeira (1983), Benjamin Highton (1997), Besley and Case (2003), and Falaschetti (2003) reported evidence that registration closing-dates significantly influence electoral mobility.

In this light, *EDR* appears to satisfy at least a minimal requirement for being a valid instrument. However, for associated inference to be accurate, *EDR* must also be "excludable"; that is, *EDR* must relate to *Loops* only through its relationship with *Turnout*. Besley and Case (2003, Table 16) developed support for this hypothesis via evidence that states randomly received the election-day registration "treatment". Here, *EDR* appears unrelated to changes in either legislatures' political composition or states' demographic characteristics.[27]

[26] *EDR* equals 1 for states where prospective voters can register on the day of an election. In the present sample, *EDR* states are Idaho, Maine, Minnesota, New Hampshire, Wisconsin, and Wyoming. Because North Dakota does not require registration, it is also treated as being a member of this group. Falaschetti (2005) also followed Benjamin Highton (1997) by coding *EDR* to equal one only for states that are early adopters of this electoral institution (i.e., North Dakota, Maine, Minnesota, and Wisconsin). Inference from this alternative coding is qualitatively identical to that reported here.

[27] Falaschetti (2005) also developed evidence from an over-identification test that *EDR* satisfies the exclusion restriction in the present application.

Gaining some satisfaction about our instrument's integrity, we can go forward in using it to calculate the USSIV coefficient estimate on *Turnout*. Fig. 3.2 reports the bootstrapped distribution of this estimate.

**Fig. 3.2** Bootstrapped distribution of the USSIV coefficient estimate on *Turnout*

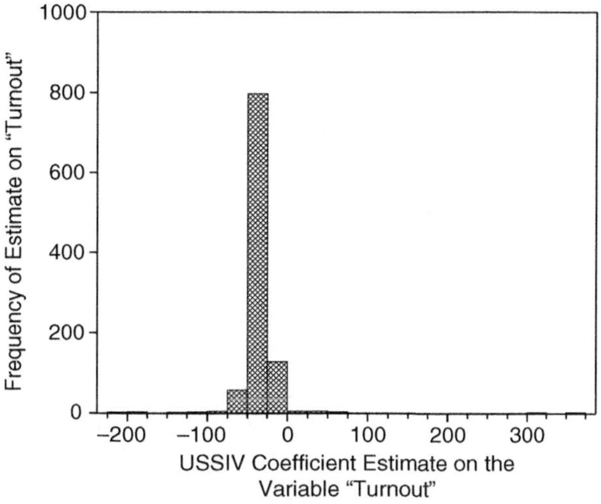


| | |
|---|---|
| Re-Samples | 1,000 |
| Mean | –35.10 |
| Standard Deviation | 23.04 |
| Upper-Bound 90% Confidence Interval | –19.58 |
| Lower-Bound 90% Confidence Interval | –51.25 |
| Maximum | 370.82 |
| Minimum | –215.76 |

The bootstrapped distribution's mean (i.e., –35.10) implies that the bias-corrected estimate of *Turnout*'s coefficient is essentially identical to its OLS counterpart from a similar specification in Table 3.4 (–35.89 in regression (8)). In addition, despite the USSIV estimator's inefficiency, inference that is available from the associated confidence intervals continues to support the hypothesis that the *Loops–Turnout* relationship is large and negative. The hypothesis that the bootstrapped distribution's mean equals zero, for example, can be rejected at any reasonable level of confidence ($t$-statistic = –48.17).

## 3.4 Conclusion

We started this chapter by making a coarse evaluation of our Chapter 1 hypotheses; that is, looking at how different proxies for economic performance correlate with a proxy for economic performance. These correlations appear to be considerable in magnitude and negative, consistent with the hypothesis that democratic governance has weakened economic performance in an important economic sector. We were also able to gain confidence that these correlations are not spurious. Indeed, across numerous alternative estimation strategies, this relationship appears to have a large causal component to it.

Concluding Part I of this book, we have a generally applicable model of how democratic governance can affect economic performance, and a solid set of empirical results that the potential for this type of governance to weaken performance is more than a theoretical curiosity. We appear to be well equipped, then, to think carefully about how democracy, at various levels of governance, affects economic performance, and turn our efforts in that direction in Part II.

## 3.5 Appendix A

Descriptions of variables

| Variable | Description | Source |
|---|---|---|
| Loops | Loops per 1,000 households that incumbent local exchange carriers (ILECs), subject to price cap regulation, maintained on 31 December 2000 | Trends in Telephone Service 2002 (Table 8.2) |
| Contribution Limit | Equals 1 if 2000 state campaign finance law prohibited regulated utilities from contributing to state level candidates | Feigenbaum and Palmer (2000) |
| Education | Percent of 1990 population, 25 years and older, that graduated high school | Geospatial and Statistical Data Center (GEOSTAT) |
| Income | 1990 median household income (in thousands) | Geospatial and Statistical Data Center (GEOSTAT) |
| Age 65 years | Percent of 1990 population aged 65 years and over | Geospatial and Statistical Data Center (GEOSTAT) |
| Clinton | Percent of 1992 general election ballots for the Democrat presidential nominee, Bill Clinton | Federal Election Commission 2003 |
| Population density | Population per square mile | Geospatial and Statistical Data Center (GEOSTAT) |

## 3.6 Appendix B

Leveraging information about selection on observables to estimate the potential for omitted variables bias

| State | Loops | Contribution Limit | Education | Income | Age 65 years | Clinton | Population Density |
|---|---|---|---|---|---|---|---|
| Alabama | 1,546 | 0 | 66.9 | 28.7 | 13.0 | 40.9 | 81.5 |
| Arkansas | 1,200 | 0 | 66.3 | 25.4 | 14.9 | 53.2 | 46.0 |
| California | 2,270 | 0 | 76.2 | 40.6 | 10.5 | 46.0 | 198.1 |
| Colorado | 2,240 | 0 | 84.4 | 35.9 | 10.0 | 40.1 | 33.4 |
| Delaware | 2,420 | 0 | 77.5 | 40.3 | 12.1 | 43.5 | 353.4 |
| Florida | 2,199 | 0 | 74.4 | 32.2 | 18.3 | 39.0 | 250.0 |
| Idaho | 1,999 | 0 | 79.7 | 29.5 | 12.0 | 28.4 | 12.9 |
| Illinois | 1,889 | 0 | 76.2 | 38.7 | 12.6 | 48.6 | 208.9 |
| Indiana | 1,715 | 0 | 75.6 | 34.1 | 12.6 | 36.8 | 157.7 |
| Iowa | 1,391 | 0 | 80.1 | 31.7 | 15.4 | 43.3 | 50.2 |
| Kansas | 1,695 | 0 | 81.3 | 33.0 | 13.9 | 33.7 | 30.7 |
| Louisiana | 1,613 | 0 | 68.3 | 26.3 | 11.1 | 45.6 | 98.2 |
| Maine | 1,557 | 0 | 78.8 | 32.4 | 13.3 | 38.8 | 40.1 |
| Maryland | 2,244 | 0 | 78.4 | 45.0 | 10.8 | 49.8 | 503.0 |
| Massachusetts | 2,015 | 0 | 80.0 | 44.4 | 13.6 | 47.5 | 764.6 |
| Michigan | 1,832 | 0 | 76.8 | 36.7 | 12.0 | 43.8 | 166.1 |
| Missouri | 1,720 | 0 | 73.9 | 31.8 | 14.0 | 44.1 | 75.3 |
| Nebraska | 1,496 | 0 | 81.8 | 31.6 | 14.2 | 29.4 | 20.8 |
| Nevada | 2,795 | 0 | 78.8 | 35.8 | 10.6 | 37.4 | 12.2 |
| New Mexico | 1,777 | 0 | 75.1 | 27.6 | 10.7 | 45.9 | 13.0 |
| New York | 1,949 | 0 | 74.8 | 39.7 | 13.1 | 49.7 | 383.5 |
| Ohio | 1,581 | 0 | 75.7 | 34.4 | 12.9 | 40.2 | 269.1 |
| Oregon | 1,853 | 0 | 81.5 | 32.3 | 13.8 | 42.5 | 31.0 |
| South Carolina | 1,473 | 0 | 68.3 | 30.8 | 11.4 | 39.9 | 119.7 |
| Texas | 2,110 | 0 | 72.1 | 31.6 | 10.1 | 37.1 | 67.5 |
| Utah | 2,190 | 0 | 85.1 | 33.2 | 8.7 | 24.7 | 22.0 |
| Vermont | 1,711 | 0 | 80.8 | 34.8 | 11.8 | 46.1 | 61.8 |
| Virginia | 2,061 | 0 | 75.2 | 38.2 | 10.8 | 40.6 | 161.5 |
| Washington | 1,899 | 0 | 83.8 | 36.8 | 11.8 | 43.4 | 77.2 |
| Arizona | 2,267 | 1 | 78.7 | 32.2 | 13.0 | 36.5 | 33.7 |
| Connecticut | 2,054 | 1 | 79.2 | 49.2 | 13.6 | 42.2 | 676.8 |
| Georgia | 1,850 | 1 | 70.9 | 33.5 | 10.1 | 43.5 | 116.9 |
| Kentucky | 1,468 | 1 | 64.6 | 27.0 | 12.7 | 44.6 | 94.5 |
| Minnesota | 1,692 | 1 | 82.4 | 36.9 | 12.5 | 43.5 | 56.1 |
| Mississippi | 1,488 | 1 | 64.3 | 24.4 | 12.5 | 40.8 | 55.7 |
| Montana | 1,276 | 1 | 81.0 | 28.0 | 13.3 | 37.6 | 5.6 |
| New Hampshire | 1,949 | 1 | 82.2 | 41.6 | 11.2 | 38.9 | 124.3 |
| New Jersey | 2,475 | 1 | 76.7 | 47.6 | 13.4 | 43.0 | 1,054.1 |
| North Carolina | 1,772 | 1 | 70.0 | 31.5 | 12.1 | 42.7 | 140.3 |
| North Dakota | 964 | 1 | 76.7 | 28.7 | 14.2 | 32.2 | 9.2 |
| Oklahoma | 1,546 | 1 | 74.6 | 28.6 | 13.5 | 34.0 | 46.7 |

(continued)

| State | Loops | Contribution Limit | Education | Income | Age 65 years | Clinton | Population Density |
|---|---|---|---|---|---|---|---|
| Pennsylvania | 1,672 | 1 | 74.7 | 34.9 | 15.4 | 45.1 | 267.6 |
| Rhode Island | 1,748 | 1 | 72.0 | 39.2 | 15.0 | 47.0 | 958.2 |
| South Dakota | 1,066 | 1 | 77.1 | 27.6 | 14.7 | 37.1 | 9.3 |
| Tennessee | 1,678 | 1 | 67.1 | 29.5 | 12.7 | 47.1 | 121.9 |
| West Virginia | 1,487 | 1 | 66.0 | 25.6 | 15.0 | 48.4 | 75.1 |
| Wisconsin | 1,452 | 1 | 78.6 | 35.1 | 13.3 | 41.1 | 91.9 |
| Wyoming | 1,577 | 1 | 83.0 | 32.2 | 10.4 | 34.0 | 4.8 |
| Mean (All) | 1,790 | 0.4 | 76.0 | 33.9 | 12.7 | 41.2 | 171.9 |
| Limit = 0 | 1,877 | 0.0 | 76.8 | 34.3 | 12.4 | 41.4 | 148.6 |
| Limit = 1 | 1,657 | 1.0 | 74.7 | 33.3 | 13.1 | 41.0 | 207.5 |
| Sum | NA | 19 | NA | NA | NA | NA | NA |

## 3.7 Appendix C

Ordinary least squares (OLS) coefficient estimates of a proxy for democratic governance (*Contribution Limit*) and controls on a proxy for economic performance (the dependent variable, *Loops*). Standard errors are White heteroskedasticity-consistent

| Variable | (A) Coefficient | SE | (B) Coefficient | SE | (C) Coefficient | SE |
|---|---|---|---|---|---|---|
| Constant | 2,416.40 | 759.89*** | 2,297.95 | 735.58*** | 2,938.64 | 495.35*** |
| Contribution Limit | −175.23 | 94.70* | −152.23 | 88.53* | −155.40 | 49.93*** |
| Education | −12.53 | 12.41 | −7.72 | 11.34 | −9.66 | 6.92 |
| Income | 45.07 | 17.28** | 36.75 | 15.49** | 30.74 | 8.09*** |
| Age 65 years | −51.77 | 37.83 | −53.97 | 33.23 | −90.18 | 16.10*** |
| Clinton | −11.49 | 8.71 | −11.61 | 8.31 | −7.95 | 5.08 |
| Pop Density | 0.00 | 0.29 | 0.09 | 0.27 | 0.30 | 0.18* |
| Fortune 500 | −0.15 | 2.80 | | | | |
| Business Lines | | | 0.04 | 0.04 | | |
| $N$ | 48 | | 48 | | 42 | |
| $R^2$ | 0.55 | | 0.56 | | 0.81 | |
| Adjusted $R^2$ | 0.47 | | 0.48 | | 0.77 | |
| $\bar{y}$ | 1,789.98 | | 1,789.98 | | 1,777.15 | |
| $\sigma_y$ | 369.45 | | 369.45 | | 319.11 | |
| $F$-statistics | 6.90 | | 7.32 | | 24.10 | |
| Probability ($F$-statistics) | 0.00 | | 0.00 | | 0.00 | |

∗∗∗, ∗∗, and ∗ indicate confidence at the 99, 95, and 90% levels, respectively.

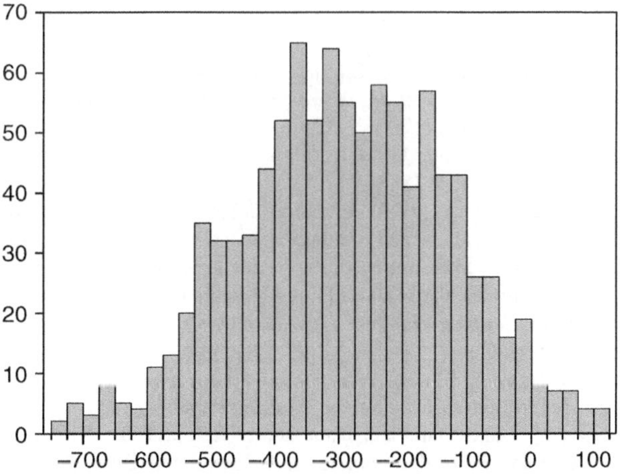


Frequency of OLS coefficient estimates on *Contribution Limit* when potentially influential observations are deleted from the dataset (Dependent variable = *Loops*)

## References

Abel, Jaison R. (2002). Entry into regulated monopoly markets: The development of a competitive fringe in the local telephone industry. *Journal of Law & Economics*, 45(2, Part 1), 289–316.

Alesina, Alberto and Guido Tabellini (1990). A positive theory of fiscal deficits and government debt. *Review of Economic Studies*, 57(3), 403–414.

Alesina, Alberto and Guido Tabellini (2007). Bureaucrats or politicians? Part I: A single policy task. *American Economic Review*, 97(1), 169–179.

Altonji, Joseph G., Todd E. Elder, and Christopher R. Taber (2005). Selection on observed variables: Assessing the effectiveness of catholic schools. *Journal of Political Economy*, 113(1), 151–184.

Angrist, Joshua D. and Alan B. Krueger (1991). Does compulsory school attendance affect schooling and earnings? *Quarterly Journal of Economics*, 106(4), 979–1014.

Angrist, Joshua D. and Alan B. Krueger (1995). Split-sample instrumental variables estimates of the return to schooling. *Journal of Business and Economic Statistics*, 13(2), 225–235.

Angrist, Joshua D. and Alan B. Krueger (2001). Instrumental variables and the search for identification: From supply and demand to natural experiments. *Journal of Economic Perspectives*, 15(4), 69–85.

Arnold, R. Douglas (1991). *The Logic of Congressional Action*. New Haven and London: Yale University Press.

Averch, Harvey and Leland L. Johnson (1962). Behavior of the firm under regulatory constraint. *American Economic Review*, 52(5), 1052–1069.

Bailey, Michael (2004). The (sometimes surprising) consequences of societally unrepresentative contributors on legislative responsiveness. *Business and Politics*, 6(3), 1–34.

Besley, Timothy and Anne Case (2003). Political institutions and policy choices: Evidence from the United States. *Journal of Economic Literature*, 41(1), 7–73.

Besley, Timothy and Stephen Coate (2003). Elected versus appointed regulators: Theory and evidence. *Journal of the European Economic Association*, 1(5), 1176–1206.

Brock, Gerald W. (1994). *Telecommunications Policy for the Information Age*. Cambridge and London: Harvard University Press.

Corrado, Anthony (2000). *Campaign Finance Reform: Beyond the Basics*. New York: The Century Foundation.

Corrado, Anthony, Thomas E. Mann, Daniel R. Ortiz, Trevor Potter, and Frank J. Sorauf (1997). *Campaign Finance Reform: A Sourcebook*. Washington, DC: Brookings Institution Press.

Council of State Governments (1999). *The Book of the States, 1998–99 Edition, Volume 32*. Lexington, KY: Council of State Governments.

Crandall, Robert W. and Hal J. Singer (2007). Telecom time warp. *Wall Street Journal*, July 11, A15.

Falaschetti, Dino (2003). Can latent groups influence policy decisions? The case of telecommunications policy. *Journal of Law, Economics, & Organization*, 19(1), 83–105.

Falaschetti, Dino (2005). Can electoral mobility diminish economic performance? Evidence from the US telecommunications sector. SSRN Working Paper, October 11. doi: 10.2139/ssrn.413583

Falaschetti, Dino (2007). Electoral accountability and consumer monopsonists: Evidence from elected vs. appointed regulators. SSRN Working Paper, July 24. doi: 10.2139/ssrn.645401.

Federal Election Commission. www.fec.gov. Accessed 31 July 2003.

Feigenbaum, Edward D. and James A. Palmer (2000). *Campaign Finance Law 2000: A Summary of State Campaign Finance Laws with Quick Reference Charts*. Washington, DC: Federal Election Commission.

Gelbach, Jonah (2004). When do covariates matter? And by how much? University of Maryland, Department of Economics, Working Paper.

Geospatial and Statistical Data Center (GEOSTAT). Charlottesville, VA: University of Virginia Library. *fisher.lib.virginia.edu*. Accessed 2003 July 31.

Gilbert, Richard J. and David M. Newbery (1994). The dynamic efficiency of regulatory constitutions. *RAND Journal of Economics*, 25(4), 538–554.

Greenberger, Robert S. (2003). Supreme court appears divided on campaign-finance measure. *Wall Street Journal*, September 9, A3, A18.

Hahn, Jinyong and Jerry Hausman (2002). Weak instruments: Diagnosis and cures in empirical econometrics. Mimeo, MIT, December.

Hanssen, F. Andrew (2004). Is there a politically optimal level of judicial independence? *American Economic Review*, 94(3), 712–729.

Hatfield, John and Gerard Miquel (2006). Multitask political agency. Working paper, Stanford University Graduate School of Business.

Hausman, Jerry (1997). Valuation and the effect of regulation on new services in telecommunications. *Brookings Papers on Economic Activity: Microeconomics*.

Henisz, Witold J. and Bennet A. Zelner (2001). The institutional environment for telecommunications investment. *Journal of Economics and Management Strategy*, 10(1), 123–148.

Highton, Benjamin (1997). Easy registration and voter turnout. *Journal of Politics*, 59(2), 565–575.

Holburn, Guy L. F. and Pablo T. Spiller (2002). Interest group representation in administrative institutions: The impact of consumer advocates and elected commissioners on regulatory policy in the United States. University of California Energy Institute (UCEI), Energy Policy and Economics Working Paper.

Jolis, Anne (2007). EU telecom regulation may hurt invest in new tech – report. *Dow Jones Newswires*. online.wsj.com. Accessed 14 September 2007.

Levitt, Steven D. and James M. Poterba (1999). Congressional distributive politics and state economic performance. *Public Choice*, 99(1–2), 185–216.

Levy, Brian and Pablo T. Spiller (1994). The institutional foundations of regulatory commitment: A comparative analysis of telecommunications regulation. *Journal of Law, Economics, and Organization*, 10(2), 201–246.

Noll, Roger G. (1986). State regulatory responses to competition and divestiture in the telecommunications industry. In Ronald E. Grieson (Ed.), *Antitrust and Regulation*, (pp. 165–200) Lexington, MA: Lexington Books.

Panteghini, Paolo M. and Carlo Scarpa (2003). Irreversible investments and regulatory risk. CESifo Working Paper No. 934.

Patterson, Samuel C. and Gregory A. Caldeira (1983). Getting out the vote: Participation in gubernatorial elections. *American Political Science Review*, 77(3), 675–689.

Persson, Torsten and Lars E. O. Svensson (1989). Why a stubborn conservative would run a deficit: Policy with time inconsistent preferences. *Quarterly Journal of Economics*, 104(2), 325–345.

Pindyck, Robert S. (2003). Mandatory unbundling and irreversible investment in telecom networks. MIT Sloan School of Management Working Paper 4452–03 (December).

Riker, William (1980). Implications from the disequilibrium of majority rule for the study of institutions. *American Political Science Review*, 74, 432–446.

Sankar, U. (1972). Investment behavior in the US electric utility industry, 1949–1968. *Bell Journal of Economics and Management Science*, 3(2), 645–664.

Sappington, David E. M. (2002). Price regulation and incentives. In Martin E. Cave, Sumit K. Majumdar, and Ingo Vogelsang (Eds.), *Handbook of Telecommunications Economics, Volume 1* (pp. 225–293). Amsterdam: Elsevier Science B.V.

Smart, Susan R. (1994). The consequences of appointment methods and party controls for telecommunications pricing. *Journal of Economics and Management Strategy*, 3(2), 301–323.

Spiller, Pablo T. (1996). Institutions and commitment. *Industrial and Corporate Change*, 5(2), 421–452.

Squeo, Anne Marie and Shawn Young (2004). Court overturns rules governing local telephone competition. *Wall Street Journal*, March 3, A1, A12.

*Trends in Telephone Service* (2002). Washington, DC: Federal Communications Commission. Available at http://www.fcc.gov/wcb/iatd/stats.html. Accessed 31 July 2003.

Wallsten, Scott (2007). Towards effective US broadband policies. Progress & Freedom Foundation Progress on Point Paper No. 14.7.

Wolfinger, Raymond E. and Steven J. Rosenstone (1980). *Who Votes?* New Haven: Yale University Press.

# Part II
# Implications for Political Bureaucracy, Competition Law, and Business Organization

# Chapter 4
# Politics

## Electoral Accountability, Credible Commitments, and Distributive Pressures

*Hence it is that such [pure] democracies have ever been spectacles of turbulence and contention; have ever been found incompatible with personal security or the rights of property.*
Madison, *Federalist X.*

Early on, Madison appreciated the fundamental difficulties that an accountable democracy must contend with and perhaps the impossibility of addressing those difficulties in a universally appealing manner. Contemporary social scientists formalized Madison's insights, confirming that these difficulties can indeed create inescapable "quandaries" – choice situations where every alternative contains unpleasant components (Schofield 2008).

For Part I of this book, those choice situations involved how much influence producers and consumers should exercise in deciding an important dimension of competition policy, namely that which governs the US telecommunications sector. There, our quandary involved creating channels through which producers can exercise a stronger policy voice (and thus risking an unproductive increase in what is commonly referred to as economic power) or closing off those channels in a more democratically appealing manner (but facilitating populist takings). Part II of this book expands this method of analysis to better understand how democratic accountability can more generally go too far in politics, law, and business.

Our analytical framework from Part I lets us see how economic performance suffers when influential electorates cannot credibly commit to fulfill policy agreements or forego redistributive takings. This chapter builds on the same channels to consider how electoral accountability can make politics, in Madison's words, "spectacles of turbulence and contention" and "incompatible with personal security or the rights of property." Appreciating how accountability in politics gives rise to such risks will then let us see how various "undemocratic" features of political organization, such as the independence of central banks, may yield the considerable social benefit of productively addressing constitutional quandaries.

D. Falaschetti, *Democratic Governance and Economic Performance*, Studies in Public Choice 14, DOI 10.1007/978-0-387-78707-7_4,

## 4.1 Electoral Accountability Can Weaken Policy Commitments: The Case of Monetary Policy

The proposition that democratic governance can weaken economic performance is perhaps easiest to appreciate in its application to monetary policy. What would happen if we voted for monetary policy agents (central bankers) like we vote for fiscal policy agents (legislators)? Such a reform would certainly make monetary policy more democratic. But would it also weaken economic performance by letting us more readily fund public goods and services by printing money?[1]

It is tempting to think we could stop ourselves from such inflationary policies and thus only enjoy the benefits of this democratic reform. But neither theory nor evidence supports the hypothesis that "accountable" central banks can credibly commit to a stable currency. Rather, accountable monetary authorities regularly buckle to democratic pressures, changing policy course at opportune times. The consequent deterioration in commitment capacity can lead to systematically looser monetary policy, higher inflation, and thus weaker economic performance.[2]

The problem here is well known and fundamental – policies that are mutually agreeable early on eventually create advantages for certain individuals at the expense of others. Individuals whose bargaining positions improve as policies play out, then, can do better by breaking their promises. Even more, the very prospect of this type of opportunism weakens commitments to optimal policies in the first place – actions that everyone at the start agrees are optimal are inconsistent with what is optimal for some down the road.

To discourage this breakdown, organizations can insulate individuals from pressures to opportunistically pursue benefits, or increase the cost of acting in an opportunistic manner. In either case, those individuals will be seen as less accountable, but economic performance will improve as long as the gain in policy commitment outweighs the increase in agency costs.

### *4.1.1 The Problem of Time Inconsistency, in Principle*

To see this "time inconsistency" problem more clearly and how insulation from democratic pressures can productively address it, consider the following excerpt from the folk song "Gallows Pole":[3]

**Accused to the hangman:** Hangman, hangman, hold it a little while, I think I see my brother coming, riding a many mile.

[1] This section builds on Falaschetti (2002) and Falaschetti and Orlando (2008).

[2] Hamilton (2008) observed that "(t)he ability to create money to pay for whatever you might deem worthwhile is one that few human beings are capable of exercising responsibly."

[3] These lyrics come from the legendary rock band, Led Zeppelin's, cover of the song.

**Accused to the brother:** Brother, did you get me some silver? Did you get a little gold? What did you bring me, my brother, to keep me from the Gallows Pole?

**Brother to the accused:** Brother, I brought you some silver, I brought a little gold, I brought a little of everything to keep you from the Gallows Pole.

**Hangman to the accused:** Your brother brought me silver . . . But now I laugh and pull so hard . . . see you swinging on the Gallows Pole!

Early in the song, the "hangman" and "accused" implicitly agree to a deal where the accused pays a bribe and the hangman releases the accused. As the song illustrates, however, the hangman eventually finds it attractive to renege on this mutually beneficial agreement – once he receives the bribe, the hangman does better for himself by breaking the agreement and going forward with the hanging.

This type of change in bargaining power as agreements play out discourages policies that, evaluated before the fact, are "optimal" or "efficient" in the sense of exhausting opportunities to make someone better off without taking away from others. And this problem is not an academic curiosity. Rather, because parties to transactions are almost certain to realize variation in their bargaining position as different responsibilities come due, optimal policies are frequently time inconsistent. The following game tree illustrates the nature of this problem (Fig. 4.1).[4]

Evaluated from the game's starting node, the actions (*Bribe*, *Don't Hang*) induce an optimal outcome. If the players could follow through on these actions, each

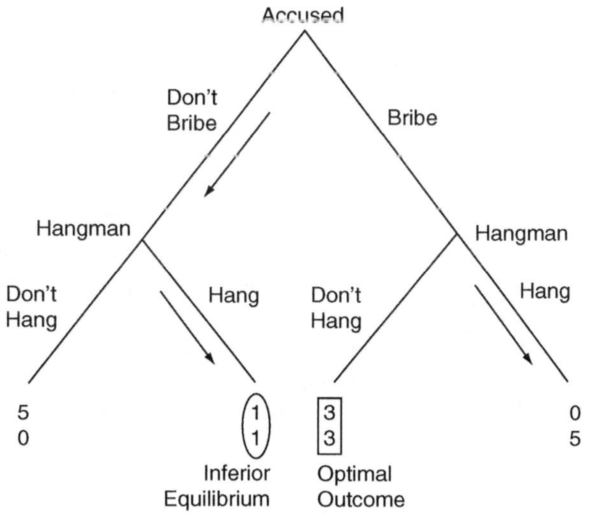


**Fig. 4.1** Optimal policy in the hangman game is inconsistent

[4]Payoffs to all possible combinations of actions are reported at the bottom of the game tree and follow the convention that the top payoff goes to the first mover – the accused in this example.

would receive a payoff of three. And note that, evaluated at this outcome, neither player's payoff can be improved without taking away from the other. In this sense, a policy that would implement the actions (*Bribe*, *Don't Hang*) is efficient.

But notice that, once the *Accused* chooses an action (any action!), the *Hangman's* best response is to *Hang*. If the *Accused* chooses *Don't Bribe*, then playing the action of *Hang* produces a payoff of one for the *Hangman* (versus zero if he chooses *Don't Hang*). And if the *Accused* instead started by choosing to *Bribe*, then the *Hangman* would again do better by hanging (and thus realize a payoff of five rather than three). Anticipating this eventuality, the *Accused* can do better by refusing to pay the bribe in the first place. Both players strictly prefer their payoffs from (*Bribe*, *Don't Hang*), but absent institutions that facilitate commitment find themselves resting with the inferior outcome (*Don't Bribe*, *Hang*).

### 4.1.2 Time Inconsistency and Monetary Policy

The hangman game illustrates how discretion to make the best choice at each stage of an agreement can, paradoxically, foreclose opportunities to enjoy mutual benefits. But it is this very type of discretion to do what is best that can cause democratic governance to produce the worst. Democratic governance changes course when doing so improves the welfare of electoral principals. By weakening political pressures to make such changes, however, insulating monetary authorities from democratic procedures would allow for stronger policy commitments and thus be a more productive governance strategy in the face of time inconsistency problems.

To see this attractive feature of undemocratic processes, consider a situation where voters are interested in how monetary policy will unfold and thus put considerable effort into anticipating policy developments.[5] And for the sake of illustration, suppose that the process of governing monetary policy makers is as democratic as possible, in the sense that policy agents *perfectly* serve the objective of their electoral principals. Finally, let us be precise about this objective by assuming that these principals are interested in maximizing a measure of economic performance that increases with output and decreases with inflation.[6]

We can analyze this model in much the same way we solved the hangman game. In particular, we can imagine the electoral principals and monetary authority implicitly agreeing, respectively, to expect little in the way of inflation and pursue a policy that creates little inflation. But just as the hangman's best action becomes inconsistent with the optimal policy after the accused takes an action, the central bank's best response becomes inconsistent after electoral constituents form expectations about inflation.

[5]This interest appears considerable in light of how prominently the speeches, testimony, and even day-to-day actions of Federal Reserve officers are featured in news media.

[6]Falaschetti and Orlando (2008) reviewed a more formal, though qualitatively identical, illustration of how time inconsistency creates problems for monetary policy.

In this latter case, the monetary authority can better serve its objective by inflating as soon as constituents form *any* expectation about how prices are going to change. Notice that, when constituents expect little in the way of inflation, an inflationary policy can boost economic output by, for example, temporarily reducing the "real" (after-inflation) cost of production factors like labor. And in a symmetric manner, if constituents instead anticipate inflation, then economic output would receive a negative shock unless monetary policy accommodates that expectation.[7]

The monetary authority thus pursues an inflationary policy for *any* expectation that its constituents form. Importantly, this departure from the original agreement to "expect little inflation and create little inflation" does not come from the authority departing from what the electorate wants. Rather, it emerges from policy agents doing exactly what the electorate wants *after* inflation-expectations are formed - take actions to maximize output.

Democratic governance, by requiring the monetary authority to do what is best at each stage of the agreement, fundamentally weakens the authority's commitment to optimal monetary policy. This "game theoretic" illustration highlights a real paradox – society can find itself stuck on an inferior outcome even if its political agent *dutifully* attempts to maximize social welfare. Moreover, it points at a potential for undemocratic forms of organization to, in a sense, save society from itself.

To preview this potential, consider what would have happened if our policy agents were institutionally tied to a policy that focused on price stability and ignored what constituents ultimately care about – output. In this version of the monetary policy game, our constituents would have rationally expected low inflation, our policy agents would have mechanically fulfilled this expectation, and society would have enjoyed a level of welfare in excess of what results from a non-committal (but accountable) policy maker.[8] By taking away the policy agent's incentive to dutifully increase output whenever it can, delegating authority to an unaccountable authority can strengthen commitments to the optimal policy!

### 4.1.3 Unaccountable Monetary Policy Can Be More Consistent

Whether a policy is optimal depends on when we evaluate it. Mutually agreeable strategies rely on obligations being fulfilled in the future. And oftentimes, those obligations look less attractive when we are eventually asked to fulfill them than they did when we originally made the agreement. This change does *not* result from new information becoming available over time or from the preferences of policy

[7]Notice that, unless monetary policy accommodates expectations in this case, the real cost of production factors can temporarily increase.

[8]An alternative to this institutional remedy is to task the monetary authority with increasing output and ask society to fool itself into believing that such an arrangement does not create perverse policy incentives. Individual members of society can do better for themselves, however, by constructively anticipating high inflation when others are irrationally (but charitably) expecting low inflation. In the end, society will thus tend toward rational expectations about inflation.

makers and constituents diverging, but rather from how past actions change subsequent bargaining positions. As such, time inconsistency is a widespread and fundamental problem that can leave even well-intentioned individuals able to commit to only sub-optimal policies.

In this section, we will further investigate how delegating policy to an insulated monetary authority can productively address this problem. Vickers (1985, p. 138) generically characterized this strategy as follows:

> If control of my decision is in the hands of an agent whose preferences are different from my own, I may nevertheless prefer the results to those that would come about if I took my own decisions.

What Vickers, and others, helped discover is that a difference in preferences can let "imperfect agents" more credibly promise actions that serve the principal's best interest. To maximize profits, for example, an incumbent firm's management might threaten to sharply drop prices whenever a competitor attempts to enter the market. But such a threat would lack credibility if incumbent management was duty-bound to pursue its principal's profit-maximizing objective. Indeed, rather than inflict economic damage on itself, the profit-maximizing manager would do better by avoiding a price war. In this case, agent-accountability weakens promises that could have served the principal's interests.

To circumvent such dilemmas, owners might do better not by hiring managers who faithfully pursue their interests but rather by hiring "imperfect" agents. Managers who focus on market share, for example, are imperfect in the sense that their objective differs from the profit-maximizing goal of owners. But these managers can also credibly promise to defensive measures and thus ultimately generate greater profits than would a more accountable agent.[9]

This type of organizational strategy can, and does, also serve more productive goals. Delegating monetary policy to an authority that cares more about inflation than output per se is an important example. Notice that the agent's objective under this strategy departs from what electoral principals "really" want, namely low inflation and high output. But this "imperfection" lets the monetary authority credibly commit to low inflation and thus indirectly strengthens economic performance.

To be sure, we saw earlier in this chapter that a perfect monetary agent has trouble committing to a low inflation policy (since opportunistic inflation can boost output). But because the imperfect agent that we have proposed can more credibly commit against inflating, electoral principals have a better reason to expect low inflation. The resulting price stability, in turn, contributes to a strengthening of economic

[9]Alan Gibbard (1973) and Mark Satterthwaite (1975) showed that the benefits from this sort of strategic delegation are robust to the particulars of Vickers' (1985) example. Roughly, the "Gibbard–Satterthwaite theorem" says that truthfully revealing one's preferences is almost never a dominant strategy (i.e., there almost always exist opponent strategies that encourage players to act in a less than truthful manner). But notice that delegating authority to a perfect agent essentially reveals the principal's true preferences. And since making such a revelation is almost never "dominant" (i.e., the best action that one can play, regardless of what one's opponent does), hiring a perfect agent can almost never be dominant.

performance. By downplaying an important but eventually inconsistent dimension of what principals really want, an "unaccountable" agent can do a better job of satisfying the principals' objectives.[10]

This insight enjoys considerable scientific support. In a series of influential papers, for example, Kenneth Rogoff (1985, 1987) showed that delegating monetary authority to a "conservative" banker can mitigate the time inconsistency problem. In Rogoff's model, society hires an agent whose preference for inflation is considerably weaker than that of the median voter.[11] To the extent that this agent can be expected to remain in office, then, society can rationally anticipate a policy that focuses more on price stability than on opportunistic output expansions. Resource allocations in this stable price environment, in turn, can be more productive than those that obtain under a monetary authority that also attempts to fine-tune economic performance.

To increase its chances of enjoying this superior equilibrium, however, society must not simply delegate monetary authority to a conservative banker, it must do so in a manner that makes circumventing that delegation costly. To be sure, delegation does not change society's preferences – while the appointed banker might be conservative, constituency preferences will not have changed. Hence, unless the cost of circumventing delegation is high enough, society will continue to have an opportunity to act on its time-inconsistent preference. Delegation without insulation does little to move a society away from the inferior discretionary equilibrium.

In practice, delegations appear to have been structured to address this difficulty; that is, they do not simply move the time-inconsistent action from opportunistically inflating to opportunistically reappointing the policy agent. Drazen (2000), for example, surveyed the literature on how central bank independence (CBI) relates to economic performance and found considerable agreement on two conclusions.[12] First, CBI negatively correlates with inflation (i.e., more independence is associated with less inflation), and this correlation is robust to how independence is measured. In addition, Drazen identified several countries (e.g., Belgium, The Netherlands) where this correlation persists despite CBI coinciding with other contending rationalizations, such as high levels of political instability and national debt. This robustness increases confidence that the correlation between CBI and low inflation evidences causation.[13]

Second, contributors to this literature have found that the low inflation associated with CBI does not systematically increase output-volatility. These results weaken concerns that a narrow focus on price stability requires banks to forego actions that

[10]Insights like these led Drazen (2000, p. 141, emphasis in original) to observe that, "Even if it were possible for the principal to appoint an agent with the same objectives, it may *not* be optimal to do so. That is, in delegating the decision over a specific policy objective, a government may come closer to achieving its preferred objective by having an agent aim for a different objective!"

[11]"Society can sometimes make itself better off by appointing a central banker who does not share the social objective function" (Rogoff 1985, p. 1169).

[12]See Drazen's (2000) chapter 5.

[13]See, however, Adam Posen (1993, 1995, 1998), who argued that CBI may simply reflect deeper societal forces (e.g., those associated with the distributional consequences of inflation).

might productively address legitimate economic shocks (e.g., a liquidity crisis after terrorist attacks). On both of these dimensions, economic performance under an "undemocratic" banker appears to be just as good, and potentially better, than what is available from a more-accountable monetary agent.

### 4.1.4 The Case of the Fed

The United States' Federal Reserve System (the Fed) illustrates how this type of organizational strategy can work in practice. The Fed persistently receives criticism for its lack of accountability. Almost every President since the foundational Federal Reserve Act of 1913, for example, has attempted to pressure the monetary authority in a substantial manner. Congress, too, has exerted considerable pressure, even passing a resolution at one point that explicitly called for looser monetary policy (Meyer 2000). Absent a well-insulated bureaucratic structure, this type of influence can lead to time-inconsistent monetary policy.

Several features of the Fed's organization have helped build this type of productive insulation. The Fed consists of 12 district banks, each of which has a president, and the Federal Reserve Board (FRB).[14] District bank presidents receive nominations from their boards of directors and confirmations from the FRB to renewable 5-year terms. The FRB, on the other hand, consists of seven governors, each of which receives a nomination from the President and confirmation from the Senate to non-renewable 14-year terms.[15] On a rotating basis, four district bank presidents combine with all seven Board members and the New York district president to comprise the Federal Open Market Committee's (FOMC) voting membership. The FOMC, in turn, proximately makes monetary policy decisions.[16]

In addition to receiving delegated authority over monetary policy, the Fed enjoys considerable insulation from political pressures. For example, it funds operations from interest earned on a portfolio of government securities.[17] But rather than being subject to the appropriations process, this portfolio largely accumulates from the Fed's open market operations (i.e., the trading of US Treasury securities through which the Fed implements monetary policy). As a consequence, Congress cannot (easily) circumvent its delegation of monetary authority by strategically manipulating bureaucratic budgets. This organizational feature thus diminishes an important channel through which monetary policy might become more accountable.

[14]Districts banks reside in Boston, New York, Philadelphia, Cleveland, Richmond (VA), Atlanta, Chicago, St. Louis, Minneapolis, Kansas City, Dallas, and San Francisco.

[15]"Board members cannot be fired, forced to resign, or voted out of office" (Waller 1992, p. 415).

[16]The FOMC meets eight times a year to determine monetary policy. "Monetary policy" refers to actions that "influence the availability and cost of money and credit to help promote national economic goals" (The Federal Reserve Board, http://www.federalreserve.gov/FOMC/default.htm; accessed on 21 September 2004).

[17]Residual earnings from this portfolio represent seignorage in the sense that the Fed transfers them to the Treasury (i.e., the US fiscal authority).

The Fed receives additional insulation from its governors serving relatively long, nonrenewable terms. One governor's term expires every other year. Each of the seven governorships thus lasts for 14 years. Moreover, governors who serve a full term cannot be reappointed. Thus, not only does delegation to the Fed receive protection from governors' terms lasting longer than do those of potentially influential political overseers, it also receives protection from those agents lacking another familiar bureaucratic control mechanism; that is, strategically manipulating the prospect of reappointment.

Despite this insulation, we should recognize that relevant institutions do not (and indeed cannot) *completely* neutralize opportunistic political forces. Rather, potentially important channels remain through which interested actors can breach the delegation of monetary authority. For example, while the prospect of reappointment seldom sways Fed governors, the original appointment process may still be influential. Interested principals might, for example, affect monetary policy by supporting the appointment of governors whose policy preferences are close to their own (rather than the conservative banker that Rogoff (1985) modeled). In this manner, the policy decisions of a subset of the FOMC (governors more so than district presidents) may be directly subject to influence at the appointment stage.

The prospect of Congressional oversight might also maintain considerable force since, while changing the "rules of the game" may be costly for Congress, the prospect is large enough for Fed officials to be considerate (Willett and Keen 1990, p. 17). This potential for ex post influence appears to gain strength from the incentives of oversight committee members. For example, Gilligan and Krehbiel (1987) argued that, if not for the ability to parlay strategic advantages into disproportionate influence, legislators would have little incentive to spend time on committee work. And as we saw above, Congress has acted in the past to curb the Fed's independence.

These channels for influence may be especially forceful when a single party controls the executive and Senate. Notice that our argument about optimal monetary policy being inconsistent did not ground itself on which party controls Congress or the executive. Rather, it built on common preferences for low inflation and high levels of output. In this framework, *any* politician can benefit from opportunistically inflating, since doing so would boost (at least temporarily) economic performance. The potential for time-inconsistent actions may thus have less to do with party identification than with the cost of acting on time-inconsistent preferences, and the cost of collectively acting on those preferences can be lower under coordinated party control.

Falaschetti (2002) developed evidence to this effect. There, when *either* party enjoys unified control, FRB governors with preferences for looser monetary policy receive appointments, and incumbent governors succumb more frequently to oversight pressures for looser policy. District bank presidents (which are further removed from these formal appointment and oversight processes), on the other hand, appear to be relatively insulated from these pressures. In this light, it is understandable why the district banks so often bear the brunt of the "lack of accountability" argument. Research findings like these also highlight, however, why that insulation is so important to maintaining integrity when political pressures are at their greatest.

## 4.2 Electoral Accountability Can Fuel Redistributive Pressures

Our Part I investigation of the telecommunications sector highlighted how accountability can weaken performance not only through dynamically inconsistent policies but also because democratic interests can create more pressure for political redistribution than for economic efficiency. This section builds on that baseline investigation by looking at how the politics of trade policy, fiscal policy, and even the judiciary can also create too much accountability in this regard.

### *4.2.1 Property Rights Can Be Stronger in Oligarchies*

> "Shall domestic manufactures be encouraged, and in what degree, by restrictions on foreign manufactures?" are questions which would be differently decided by the landed and the manufacturing classes, and probably by neither with a sole regard to justice and the public good. Madison, *Federalist X*.

As we saw in Part I, economic performance tends to be stronger when individuals can fully enjoy the benefits of their actions. In this light, understanding how governance mechanisms evolve to productively create and enforce property rights is perhaps the most fundamental goal for economic development scholarship. And contrary to many popular observations, a more accountable democracy is not always the answer.

An oligarchic society can be defined as one that concentrates political power in large-scale producers.[18] As such, oligarchies are anything but democratically accountable. But under common conditions, they can promote stronger economic performance.

By definition, oligarchic producers are a source of considerable political influence. This influence, in turn, can create a sturdy insulation from populist distributional pressures that might otherwise lead to opportunistic expropriations or excessive taxes. We saw in Part I of this book, however, that this power can also go too far, making producers better off at the expense of (rather than in addition to) consumers. Moreover, this power can discourage new firms from entering markets, effectively weakening the property rights of prospective entrepreneurs (Acemoglu 2003).

Democracy can check these latter difficulties but, as we also saw in Part I, poses the quandary of creating its own risks for economic performance. To be sure, this more widely accountable form of governance can lower barriers for new entrepreneurs. But just as oligarchies give rise to entry barriers that offset the benefits of their strong property rights, democracies give rise to distortionary taxes that work against their benefits of more competitive entry conditions (Acemoglu 2003).

How these trade-offs are settled influences which type of political organization ultimately produces better economic performance. Acemoglu (2003, p. 4) characterized this trade-off as follows:

[18] See, for example, Acemoglu (2003).

Successful economic performances will come from democracies that are relatively less redistributive, and from oligarchic societies where entry barriers are limited or where heterogeneity of productivity in entrepreneurship is relatively unimportant.

In this light, neither governance form appears to be dominant (i.e., the best form under *any* conditions) and the comparative advantage of one over the other can change as a society evolves. Perhaps as a consequence, rather than systematically outperforming more narrowly accountable forms of government, postwar democracies do not appear to have grown considerably faster than have oligarchies (Barro 1999).

Similar dynamics can also affect comparative governance advantages through the channel of foreign direct investment (FDI). FDI has been flagged as an important factor in economic development. Since the cost of enforcing international agreements is relatively high, however, and foreign investors often lack a direct channel for influencing domestic politics, this type of investment is especially prone to expropriation.

Facundo Albornoz et al. (2008) argued that, under certain conditions, democratic governance heightens this political risk. This argument formally builds on the observation that a considerable number of nationalizations and reversals of FDI occurred in early 20th century Latin America, at about the same time that populist political regimes were coming to power. During this period, FDI appears to have lowered the cost of exporting agricultural products, effectively increasing the price that land owners receive for their output. But because labor is more mobile than is land, competition in the labor market would have largely precluded this price increase from being shared through increased wages. Instead, the economic benefit of lower transport costs appears to have been largely realized by the landowners. In such cases, if democratic governments tend to rely on the mass of support that laborers can provide, and oligarchic governments tend to rely on the elite support of property owners, the distribution of FDI benefits will give democracies a weaker incentive than oligarchies to protect property rights in investment.

### *4.2.2 Deficits Can Encourage More Productive Government Spending*

The apportionment of taxes on the various descriptions of property is an act which seems to require the most exact impartiality; yet there is, perhaps, no legislative act in which greater opportunity and temptation are given to a predominant party to trample on the rules of justice. Every shilling with which they overburden the inferior number, is a shilling saved to their own pockets. Madison, *Federalist X*.

Government deficits are frequently pointed to as evidence of an unaccountable government.[19] And this lack of accountability appears to be so persistent that Congress has repeatedly proposed a "Deficit Accountability Act".[20]

[19]This section builds on Falaschetti (2008).

[20]The Act would ban automatic pay increases for Members of Congress in years that follow a Federal budget deficit. Representative Cliff Stearns (R-FL) introduced HR 229, the

Rather than strengthen economic performance, however, increasing accountability on this dimension could facilitate more redistributive and less productive government spending. Public projects require financial capital, but financial capital is not just "money" that facilitates the exchange of goods and services. Rather, it is money bundled with rights and obligations that govern economic exchange. And balanced budget spending lacks several productive governance features that are built into deficit spending.

Democrats and Republicans agree that the US government is borrowing too much.[21] But instead of reflecting widespread support for productive policy, this agreement may evidence a common incentive to redistribute wealth for political gain. Indeed, while the invisible hand of markets facilitates win-win bargains, the visible hand of government trumps efficiency by favoring a plurality of voters at others' expense. A political candidate can do better, for example, by promising net tax benefits to 51% of the electorate instead of more evenly spreading fiscal responsibilities. Rather than expand general economic opportunities as proponents suggest, balanced budget spending may simply facilitate divisive but politically attractive tax transfers.

In this light, running deficits appears to be part of the solution, not the root problem. Because voting markets tend to take from those without a voice, tax-financed spending often channels resources to politically attractive (though not always productive) uses. Financial markets, on the other hand, better reward making than they do taking. Having to fund deficits (rather than balance budgets) can thus replace political motivations to redistribute with market discipline to expand economic opportunity.

To be sure, the argument here is not that more (or less) government spending is necessarily better. Rather, it is to simply observe that financial markets, despite recent credit channel difficulties, fundamentally discipline public spending better than do voting markets. A "bridge to nowhere", on its own, will encounter considerable difficulty attracting financial capital. But the ability of voting markets to widely spread the tax costs of such unproductive projects, and concentrate the benefits onto politically attractive constituencies, is now a headline reality. By increasing the cost of purely political redistributions while supporting sound public investment, running deficits can improve government quality.

---

"Deficit Accountability Act of 2007", to the House of Representatives on 4 January 2007. As of this book's writing, the bill does not appear to have gone further than being referred to the Committee on House Administration and the Committee on Oversight and Government Reform (see The Library of Congress's "Thomas" database, http://thomas.loc.gov/cgi-bin/query/z?c110:H.R.+229:, accessed on 15 November 2008). Representative Stearns, sometimes teaming with other Members of Congress, has introduced this bill to several Congresses (e.g., see Representative Stearns' press release for the "Deficit Accountability Act of 2004" at http://www.house.gov/stearns/PressReleases/PR2004Releases/pr-040210-payraise.html, accessed 15 on November 2008).

[21] See, for example, Phillips and McKinnon (2008).

To see how this improvement works, consider a $100 spending proposal that promises to return (at most) $100 in the future. Because this project does not strengthen the public's repayment ability, financial markets will be reluctant to fund it. Doing so would be like putting $100 in the bank with the prospect of getting (at most) $100 in the future. Individual depositors do not willingly give up money in such circumstances, and financial markets are likewise reluctant to fund government spending that promises little in the way of expanding economic opportunities.

Political markets that assign tax burdens lack this discipline. Suppose, for example, that group A enjoys more political influence than does group B, and a political entrepreneur proposes to simply give $100 to group A. In cases like this one, voting markets will tend to fund the proposal as long as it asks for less than $100 in taxes from group A (or as long as group B lacks a political voice).

Even worse, rather than simply being redistributive, politically attractive tax-and-transfer projects tend to shrink economic opportunities. First, these projects encourage individuals to lobby to be counted as members of favored groups (like group A in the above illustration). Economies prosper, however, when governance institutions reward productive efforts and suffer when individuals instead spend time seeking redistributive rents. Second, taxes create a wedge between prices that buyers pay and sellers receive, and thus discourage mutually beneficial transactions. But it is mutually beneficial transactions, not zero- (or negative) sum transfers, that expand economic opportunities.

Politicians and popular media frequently argue that households must balance their budgets as motivation for governments to do the same. But while balancing budgets productively disciplines household spending, it allows for political discretion in public spending. Households face the full costs of *their own* balanced budget spending and thus tend to wisely allocate those dollars. Balancing public budgets, however, only means that aggregate tax revenues fully fund expenditures, not that individual costs align with benefits. And as the above example illustrates, politicians on *both* sides of the aisle face strong incentives to divide those who benefit from public spending from those who bear the tax cost.

To encourage a more productive investment of public resources, a funding mechanism must curb inefficient but politically rewarding discretion. While balancing budgets serves this goal for households, it does not do so for governments. In the latter case, corporations offer a more instructive comparison.

"Voters" in corporations (i.e., shareholders) readily agree to run deficits, in part because debt capital offers important advantages in governing a firm's management. Like their corporate counterparts, government bondholders put their money where their mouths are and thus help narrow the political discretion that otherwise allows for unproductive tax redistributions. While political entrepreneurs market deficit-reduction as a constructive method for living within our means, they may instead be lobbying for a method that facilitates electorally attractive, but economically destructive, increases in government spending.

Funding public expenditures through financial (rather than voting) markets can give us a better idea about the appropriate scope of government activity while encouraging a more productive employment of public resources once that scope is set. To be sure, both borrowing and taxing offer channels through which politically influential groups can tilt resources in their favor. For taxes, this redistribution largely occurs across groups within a generation, whereas debt might transfer resources from future generations to the present. But debt also embodies a number of self-policing mechanisms, whereas taxes create relatively little discipline on how productively governments spend resources.

Financial markets continually discount the potential for public spending to decrease the government's repayment ability. Deficits that would simply redistribute from future to current generations thus receive a forceful and well-timed check. Tax-financed spending avoids this discipline. Indeed, political markets give little weight to those who do not vote and thus tend to ignore the (necessarily silent) protests of those who would inherit inferior opportunities in the future from unproductive tax spending today. By benefiting a dominant coalition of current voters, that spending may nevertheless go forward (over-promising on Social Security and other entitlements may have resulted from this type of political calculus). Instead of burdening future generations, deficits give similarly interested financial markets a seat at the table today, where they can productively voice concerns about whether public spending redistributes a shrinking pie or creates new economic opportunities that can be widely shared.

Economists have long debated whether deficits matter. They do, but perhaps more for replacing voting markets that reward politically attractive redistributions with financial markets that place greater weight on productivity. Tax-funding mechanisms evaluate spending proposals against their distributional properties, not against the standard of whether public actions generally expand economic opportunities. To attract funding through debt markets, spending proposals must reasonably promise to strengthen society's repayment ability. Moreover, debt markets transparently report on the credibility of such promises by continually evaluating the price at which government obligations are traded. Having to borrow, not balance budgets, can productively discipline governments by charging a higher price for funds that would simply facilitate transfers while readily supporting public projects that strengthen economic performance.

### *4.2.3 Insulated Judges Can Seek Truths and Ignore Inefficient Distributive Pressures from Aggregating Preferences*

> Yet the parties are, and must be, themselves the judges; and the most numerous party, or, in other words, the most powerful faction must be expected to prevail. Madison, *Federalist X*.

Similar to the Fed, the US judicial branch is a well-insulated bureaucracy. Supreme Court Justices, for example, serve unlimited terms and do not face the prospect of reappointment. Unlike their banking counterparts, however, judges oftentimes stand for election and work within legislatively determined budget constraints. And through channels like these, the judiciary can face inefficient distributional pressures that weaken its ability to decide cases on the merits.

A desirable quality for a judiciary is "truth seeking", and it has long been appreciated that a panel of jurists (rather than a single judge) can help move societies in this direction. Indeed, Condorcet's 18th century "Jury Theorem" shows us how a majority rule decision-making process can arrive at better conclusions, on average, than can a single individual. In particular, as long as individuals maintain a better than 50% chance of choosing the correct alternative (e.g., guilty or not guilty), a society can achieve any level of certainty in arriving at a correct decision by making its juries large enough.

To see how this theorem works, consider a coin that has a slightly greater chance of landing on heads and notice that it can nevertheless exhibit a tendency to land on tails if we flip it only a few times. But as we repeatedly flip this coin, the probability that it will land on heads more than tails will increase. As the number of flips increases, the "true" tendency of the coin is thus revealed. Similarly, a 9-member panel has a better chance of finding the truth than does a 5-member panel, and a 101-member panel a better chance still.

But for Condorcet's theorem to work in practice, decision makers must be disinterested in what is true; that is, groups are better than individuals at aggregating what Schofield (2008) has referred to as "beliefs", not preferences. Recall our example of flipping coins and notice that we did not say anything about preferences over whether the coin tends to land on heads. Rather, our objective was simply to discover this tendency. But if realizing the coin's true tendency led to a personally favorable or unfavorable outcome, say winning or losing a bet, then we would not have been aggregating only beliefs about the truth – we would have also been aggregating preferences over what is true.

While groups have an advantage over individuals in discovering "what is",[22] however, collective, decision-making runs into difficulty when preferences enter the picture.[23] To see how, consider a model society where three individuals (1, 2, 3) have very different preferences over three policies ($x$, $y$, $z$). In particular, suppose that our first individual prefers policy $x$ to $y$ and $y$ to $z$. Likewise, suppose that individual two prefers policy $y$ to $z$ and $z$ to $x$, while individual three prefers $z$ to $x$ and $x$ to $y$. Fig. 4.2 summarizes these profiles.

| | **Individual 1** | **Individual 2** | **Individual 3** |
|---|---|---|---|
| **Most preferred policy** | $x$ | $y$ | $z$ |
| | $y$ | $z$ | $x$ |
| **Least preferred policy** | $z$ | $x$ | $y$ |

**Fig. 4.2** Majority rule does not improve upon individual decision-making when preference satisfaction replaces truth seeking as an objective

[22]James Surowiecki (2004) described this implication as the "wisdom of crowds."

[23]Norman Schofield authoritatively developed this conclusion in a more general form see, for example, Schofield (2008). We will see another application of this important insight in Chapter 6 of this book, where democratic corporate governance may lead to the unintended consequence of destabilizing business strategies.

Endowed with individual profiles like these, a democratic society may experience considerable turbulence. Notice, for example, that our modeled society prefers alternative $x$ to $y$ under majority rule (since two of the three individuals, the first and third, prefer $x$ to $y$). But this same society also prefers $y$ to $z$ (since individuals one and two prefer $y$ to $z$) and $z$ to $x$ (since individuals two and three prefer $z$ to $x$). In other words, measured through a democratically accountable mechanism like majority rule, individually rational preferences give rise to a chaotic society that prefers $x$ over $y$, $y$ over $z$, and $z$ over $x$!

Exposing judiciaries to democratic pressures can compromise a stable and efficiency-promoting process of belief aggregation, letting preferences over distribution play a more forceful role, increasing the potential for chaos, and thus weakening the prospects for a dispassionate and stable rule of law to serve as the foundation for strong economic performance. Temptations to increase this exposure, nevertheless, are strong and persistent. Indeed, even a court that is infallible with respect to the facts will see at least half of the parties coming before it leave with something other than their most preferred outcome. And when these facts tend to work against the preferences of influential groups, forces for increased accountability will grow stronger. But rather than improve performance, achieving this increase may serve politically attractive distributions at the expense of a more stable and productive rule of law.[24]

## 4.3 Conclusion: When Can Policy Benefit from Undemocratic Processes?

Thomas Schelling's (1960) groundbreaking work started a contemporary appreciation of how delegating decision-making authority to *imperfect* agents can paradoxically lead to preferable outcomes for their principals. Alberto Alesina and Guido Tabellini (2007) furthered this understanding, carefully deriving conditions under which policies from delegated bureaucrats regularly do better than those from more democratically accountable politicians.[25] These conditions include predictable electoral preferences and a considerable potential for time-inconsistency problems, both of which characterize our telecommunications application in Part I, as well as the extended political applications reviewed in this chapter. Indeed, monetary authorities must continually address the time-inconsistency problem, and identifiable

[24] A 27 November 2007 panel at the Stanford Law School (Ruling the law: judges, legislators, and the struggle for judicial independence) included former Supreme Court Justice Sandra Day O'Connor and highlighted both the long history of such risks and the possibility that they are increasing (iTunes.stanford.edu, accessed on 16 November 2008). Famous Presidents such as Thomas Jefferson, Andrew Jackson, Theodore Roosevelt, and Franklin D. Roosevelt, for example, arguably placed considerable distributive pressures on the judiciary while making it more "accountable." Contemporary democratic pressures to reign in "activist" judges appear to have encouraged Congressional threats of judicial budget cuts and impeachment, and even a state-level "jail for judges" ballot initiative to hold judges (and jurors) accountable for "erroneous" decisions.

[25] Eric Maskin and Jean Tirole (2004) developed a related analysis.

groups benefit from restricting trade, strategically assigning fiscal responsibilities, and regulating through litigation. And evidence from these applications, both formal and anecdotal, supports Alesina and Tabellini's (2007) conjecture that, as a consequence, economic performance can indeed grow stronger as governance becomes less democratic under predictable conditions.

The last two substantive chapters of this book extend this analytical framework from "macrogovernance" organizations (federal authorities) to more "microlevel" governance structures. Chapter 5 looks at how competition laws that govern producer–consumer interactions can also become overly exposed to democratic pressures. Our arguments here extend those from Part I to better understand how competition laws improve economic performance in principle, and why they regularly depart from this ideal to instead facilitate politically expedient distributions.

Chapter 6 moves to a more micro-level still, from the democratic governance of firms to governance within firms. Here, we will see that democratic corporate governance can destabilize business strategy, and otherwise create inefficient distributional pressures within the firm. These influences appear to work through the same fundamental channels that we have encountered throughout this book, and again result in considerable politico-legal risks for economic performance.

## References


Acemoglu, Daron (2003). The form of property rights: oligarchic vs. democratic societies. NBER Working Paper 10037 (October).

Albornoz, Facundo, Sebastian Galiani, and Daniel Heymann (2008). Investment and expropriation under oligarchy and democracy in a Heckscher-Ohlin world. SSRN Working Paper, http://ssrn.com/abstract=1085360.

Alesina, Alberto and Guido Tabellini (2007). Bureaucrats or politicians? Part I: a single policy task. *American Economic Review*, 97(1), 169–179.

Barro, Robert (1999). *Determinants of Economic Growth: a Cross-Country Empirical Study*. Cambridge, MA: MIT Press.

Drazen, Allan (2000). *Political Economy in Macroeconomics*. Princeton: Princeton University Press.

Falaschetti, Dino (2002). Does partisan heritage matter? The case of the Federal Reserve. *Journal of Law, Economics, and Organization*, 18(2), 488–510.

Falaschetti, Dino (2008). When deficits make sense. *Hoover Digest* (3), 72–75.

Falaschetti, Dino, and Michael J. Orlando (2008). *Money, Financial Intermediation, and Governance*. Gloucestershire: Edward Elgar Publishing.

Gibbard, Alan (1973). Manipulation of voting schemes: a general result. *Econometrica* 41(4), 587–601.

Gilligan, Thomas W. and Keith Krehbiel (1987). Collective decisionmaking and standing committees: An informational rationale for restrictive amendment procedures. *Journal of Law, Economics, and Organization* 3(3), 287–335.

Hamilton, James (2008). Central bank independence. *Econbrowser: Analysis of Current Economic Conditions and Policy*, April 13. http://www.econbrowser.com/archives/2008/04/central_bank_in.html. Accessed 13 November 2008.

Maskin, Eric and Jean Tirole (2004). The politician and the judge: accountability in government. *American Economic Review* 94(4), 1034–1054.

Meyer, Laurence H. (2000). The politics of monetary policy: balancing independence and accountability. Remarks by Federal Reserve Board Governor to the University of Wisconsin, LaCrosse,

October 24. http://www.federalreserve.gov/BOARDDOCS/SPEECHES/2000/20001024.htm. Accessed 14 November 2008.

Phillips, Michael M. and John D. McKinnon (2008). Legacy of deficits will constrain Bush's successor. *Wall Street Journal* (February 1), A3.

Posen, Adam (1993). Why central bank independence does not cause low inflation: there is no institutional fix for politics. In Richard O'Brien (Ed.), *Finance and the International Economy, Volume 7* (pp. 40–65). Oxford: Oxford University Press.

Posen, Adam (1995). Declarations are not enough: financial sector services of central bank independence. In Ben Bernanke and Julio Rotemberg (Eds.), *NBER Macroeconomics Annual 1995* (pp. 253–274). Cambridge: MIT Press.

Posen, Adam (1998). Do better institutions make better policy? *International Finance* 1(1), 173–205.

Rogoff, Kenneth (1985). The optimal degree of commitment to an inter mediate monetary target. *Quarterly Journal of Economics* 100(4), 1169–1189.

Rogoff, Kenneth (1987). Reputational constraints on monetary policy. In Karl Brunner and Allan Meltzer (Eds.), *Carnegie-Rochester Conference Series on Public Policy, Volume 26* (pp. 141–181). Amsterdam, New York, and Oxford: North-Holland Publishing Company.

Satterthwaite, Mark (1975). Strategy-proofness and Arrow's conditions. *Journal of Economic Theory* 10(2), 187–217.

Schelling, Thomas C. (1960). *The Strategy of Conflict*. Cambridge, MA and London: Harvard University Press.

Schofield, Norman J. (2008). *The Political Economy of Democracy and Tyrrany*. Munich: Oldenbourg.

Surowiecki, James (2004). *The Wisdom of Crowds*. New York: Random House, Inc.

Vickers, John (1985). Delegation and the theory of the firm. *Economic Journal*, 95(Supplement – Conference Papers), 138–147.

Waller, Christopher J. (1992). A bargaining model of partisan appointments to the central bank. *Journal of Monetary Economics* 29(3), 411–428.

Willett, Thomas D. and Edward Keen (1990). Studying the Fed: Toward a broader public choice perspective. In Thomas Mayer (Ed.), *The Political Economy of American Monetary Policy* (pp. 13–26). Cambridge: Cambridge University Press.

# Chapter 5
# Law

## Welfare Standards and Competition Policy

By methodically evaluating conventional wisdoms, our formal models from Part I of this book exposed an important source of influence on competition policy that less scientific commentaries often miss – like producers, *consumers also have an incentive to seek political advantage* and, when that advantage is realized, tend to favor themselves at others' expense. This implication follows from a consistent treatment of micro-motivations for individual choices, whether those choices are made in firms where individuals produce or in marketplaces where individuals consume. Everyone has an interest in institutions that favor themselves, even if those institutions create negative-sum games for society.

At least in principle, then, the problem of too much power rests with consumers as well as with producers. Moreover, the statistical evidence developed in Part I suggests that, rather than being an abstract possibility, at least one important economic sector is underperforming because democratic governance receives too much influence from consumers.

This chapter examines whether this type of politico-legal risk may also be weakening the performance of other important economic sectors. Recall that our models from Part I do not imply that accountability can go too far only in the telecommunications sector. Rather, they say that *any* sector in which pressure-group competition, credible commitments, or real options are salient maintains channels through which electoral groups can favor themselves at the expense of society more generally. Hence, even if these other sectors do not readily lend themselves to the kind of quasi-experimental analysis that is possible with telecommunications, they may nevertheless find themselves exposed to considerable risks from overly democratic governance.

This chapter begins by reviewing what can appear to be a reasonable objective for antitrust law and competition policy (i.e., discourage or remedy accumulations of market power), and how politico-legal forces have pointed economic sectors away from this productive end. It then offers a case study of the property insurance sector to illustrate how competition policy can instead favor consumer interests over the greater good and may have done so in economically important sectors other than telecommunications. Finally, it concludes by asking how private governance

D. Falaschetti, *Democratic Governance and Economic Performance*, Studies in Public Choice 14, DOI 10.1007/978-0-387-78707-7_5,

strategies can reduce this type of non-market risk and by arguing that lawyers and business managers can do better for themselves by helping to produce this public service.

## 5.1 Competition Policy Can Strengthen Economic Performance

Competitive markets are ideal in the sense that they do not rest until all mutually beneficial trades are discovered and completed. Economies that succeed on this margin thus enjoy an "efficient" allocation of resources – an outcome from which no one can be made better off without making someone else worse off.

Laws that economize on the cost of transacting let societies approach this ideal. "Good" laws ease the way for mutually attractive trading partners to find each other, agree on the attributes of goods and services under consideration, and, after an exchange is made, enforce the governing terms. Here, relatively little stands in the way of transactions that make at least one person happier without diminishing anyone else. When the "rule of law" succeeds on this important margin, economic performance thus tends to be strong in terms of wealth levels, growth rates, and even distribution (at least from an ex ante perspective).[1]

These implications are unsurprising to social scientists and, while they have been rigorously developed in theory and evaluated in practice, are intuitive enough to be agreeable to nonspecialists as well. The really important puzzle, then, is not so much what causes strong economic performance but rather why so many people have missed out on these opportunities for so long.

Humankind has been poor for almost all of its existence and most people are poor today. Oded Galor (2005) observed, for example, that the history of economic performance is almost entirely one of "Malthusian stagnation", with increases in output consistently outpacing increases in population for only the last 200 years or so. And even this recent welfare improvement has not been widely shared. Indeed, while some individuals were finally escaping what appeared to be perpetual stagnation, per capita income between rich and poor regions of the world was experiencing the "Great Divergence", a gap that grew from almost nothing before the year 1000 to 3:1 in 1820 and 18:1 in 2001. David Weil (2004) illustrates this astounding disparity by noting that over three-quarters of today's world population earns a below-average income, and that average is less than $8,000 per year (the poverty level for a US individual in 2007 was almost $11,000).[2]

Rationalized within the model described above, about how laws influence economic opportunities, these data suggest that "rules of the game" too often discour-

---

[1] Absent transactions costs, markets are complete. Contracts could be written before the fact, for example, to insure against outcomes that diminish one's life chances. While the standard of economic efficiency is frequently criticized for ignoring the welfare consequences of distribution, an economy with complete markets would also achieve equity in initial distributions.

[2] Source for poverty level: US Census Bureau. Poverty thresholds 2007. http: //www.census.gov/hhes/www/poverty/threshld/thresh07.html. Accessed 2008 July 22.

age (rather than facilitate) mutually beneficial exchange. This rationalization also highlights a channel through which laws can increase social welfare - by reducing the level of resources to facilitate exchange, laws can let goods and services more freely move to highly valued uses.[3]

Antitrust law and competition policy, at least on their face, work toward this ideal by preempting accumulations of market power from which inefficient trade restrictions can emerge and, if such power nevertheless accumulates, offering remedies that expand trade for the greater good. The explicit concern here is that of "monopoly" - producers commanding so much power that they can raise price above competitive levels and thus enjoy economic benefits not from mutually beneficial trades, but at the expense of consumers who exit the market when prices rise above competitive levels.

## 5.2 But Legal Ideals Must Work Within Political Constraints

The leading rationalization for why poverty (rather than prosperity) is the norm, however, is not that natural monopolists have had their way for almost all of human history. Rather, it is that individuals' rights to enjoy the product of their efforts (as well as obligations to internalize their costs) have been too weak. In an influential article, Daron Acemoglu et al. (2001, p. 1369) illustrated this rationalization as follows:

> At some level it is obvious that institutions [for private property] matter. Witness, for example, the divergent paths of North and South Korea, or East and West Germany, where one part of the country stagnated under central planning and collective ownership, while the other prospered with private property and a market economy.

In this light, the *fundamental* problem of dismal economic performance is not producers keeping too much of what they make. Rather, it is political agents taking too much on behalf of important support constituencies.[4] But instead of weakening the incentive and ability for politicians to pursue such inefficient policies, antitrust laws and competition policies can instead strengthen them.

Laws are the output of public choice processes, the distributional consequences of which create political pressures. These pressures, in turn, can trump rights and responsibilities that could have otherwise strengthened economic performance. To see this difficulty, consider a policy that promises to move an economy from a monopolistic to a competitive outcome, thereby expanding available opportunities. But notice that, if producers can do better under this type of expansion, they

---

[3]Ronald Coase (1960) is frequently credited with the seminal development of this normative legal theory. David Friedman (2000) offers an accessible explanation of the theory, as well as an interesting account of its historical development.

[4]Acemoglu (2003, p. 6) similarly observed that, while "Many studies on economic growth and the political economy of development have pointed out the costs of entry barriers . . . An even larger literature . . . focuses on the cost of redistribution."

would not have implemented anticompetitive measures in the first place. And if the existence of such measures is associated with political influence, then producers have an interest and ability to block the development of laws that would improve economic performance.[5]

Even more, producers who would otherwise find themselves in fierce competition can benefit from laws that provide insulation against market pressures for efficiency. To be sure, *general* economic performance suffers from such laws, but producers who live to see those laws enacted can operate in an environment where pressure to maintain competitive prices is weak. Here, again, *socially* desirable antitrust laws and competition policies will face strong political resistance. Considerations like these led Acemoglu (2002, p. 1) to argue that "inefficient policies and institutions are prevalent... because they serve the interests of politicians or social groups holding political power, at the expense of the society at large."

Perhaps contrary to conventional wisdom, however, this type of resistance does not emanate only from self-interested producers. Rather, consumers also have an incentive to support laws that favor themselves at others' expense. Indeed, just as producers prefer a larger share of the restricted benefits from a monopolistic economy, consumers prefer a larger share of the restricted benefits from a monopsonistic economy.[6] And while antitrust laws and competition policies formally ignore this latter type of inefficient trade restriction, evidence from Part I of this book suggests that it is an empirically important problem. The remainder of this section lays the foundation and builds a case study to further suggest that competition policy can, and does, become too accountable to consumers.

### *5.2.1 Producers Lobby for Market Power, Not Efficiency*

When general-purpose antitrust laws cannot stop unproductive accumulations of market power, specific regulations can increase consumer welfare while improving economic performance more generally. But regulations can also be more immediately exposed to political pressures than are judicially administered antitrust laws. And this exposure can cause regulation to serve distributional rather than efficiency goals (Falaschetti 2008).

Chicago School scholars famously demonstrated this phenomenon, showing how regulations can cartelize producers and thus create the very concentration of power that (at least on its face) competition policy aims to diffuse. Figure 5.1(adapted from Mueller 1989) helps us understand this argument.

In a competitive market, producers sell any and all of their output at the market-clearing price ($P_C$), and this price must equal the marginal cost of production (*MC*).

[5]Raghuram Rajan and Luigi Zingales (2003) offer an accessible and authoritative extension of this argument to the financial sector.

[6]Just as "monopoly" refers to a condition where economic power is concentrated in producers, "monopsony" refers to a condition where power is concentrated in buyers.

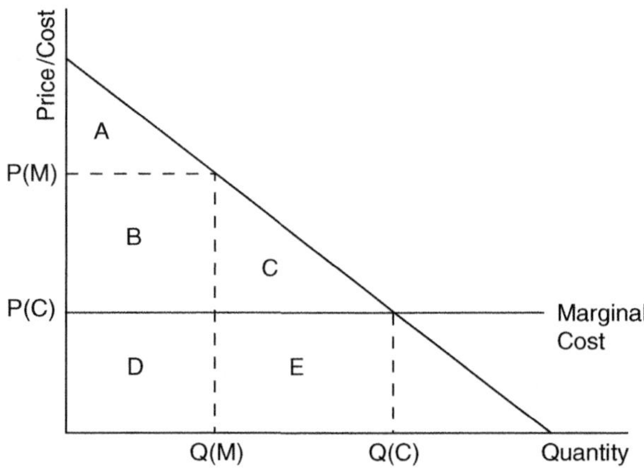


**Fig. 5.1** Distributional benefits social cost of monopoly

If these conditions did not hold, mutually beneficial trades would be available and firms would enter or exit until profit opportunities were exhausted (i.e., until $P_C = MC$).[7] Ultimately, then, competitive firms just recoup the opportunity cost of their investments (the sum of areas D and E in Fig. 5.1). Meanwhile, consumers recognize a relatively large "surplus" (i.e., the differences between their willingness-to-pay and the market price). In the present figure, the sum of the areas A, B, and C represents this surplus.

Unlike the competitive firm, the monopolist can charge a price $P_M$ that exceeds its marginal cost since, by definition, others cannot enter and participate in the positive economic profits (benefits above what is necessary to encourage production at the monopolistic level of output). By following this strategy, the monopolist transfers to itself some of the consumer surplus that would have been generated from competitive conditions (i.e., the area denoted by B). But while the monopolist improves its own lot (since it enjoys "rents", or benefits that exceed what is necessary to induce entry to this sector), it does so at the expense of social welfare by decreasing *total* surplus (the sum of areas denoted by A and B) to a level that falls below what would have emerged from a competitive process (the sum of areas denoted by A, B, and C). In this light, conventionally interpreted antitrust measures and competition policies appear to serve a *social* goal by letting consumers regain some of the deadweight loss triangle (the area denoted by C) when producers would have otherwise enjoyed economic power.

Notice, however, that whether they can accumulate market power on their own, existing firms have an interest in regulations that facilitate moving toward monop-

[7]Notice that, to the extent that price exceeds marginal cost, there exist consumers who are willing to purchase additional quantities of output for a slightly lower price (since the demand curve slopes downward) and producers who are willing to supply additional quantities (since the slightly lower price would still exceed the producers' marginal cost). Absent frictions to the contrary, these mutually beneficial transactions will continue until the market price equals the marginal cost of production.

olistic outcomes. For the stylized economy illustrated in Fig. 5.1, firms have an incentive to bid for such protection up to the area denoted by B.[8] And if the private benefits that political agents can gain from accepting such bids outweigh associated costs, then agents will work against regulations that generally expand economic opportunities and instead craft regulations that strategically serve distributional interests, even at a considerable social cost.

Sam Peltzman (1976) is frequently cited for having discovered this possibility.[9] For Peltzman, a regulator's livelihood depends on how its decisions affect the welfare not only of consumers, but also that of protection-seeking producers. In his model, regulated prices thus exhibit a tendency to settle *between* what a monopolist would charge (the protection-seeking firm's ideal price) and what a competitive firm would charge ("society's" ideal price).[10] And these competing pressures can rationalize the perhaps otherwise anomalous observation that powerful and competitive producers, alike, strenuously lobby regulators. Here, natural monopolists will lobby to *maintain* pricing-power and competitive firms will lobby to *gain* power.[11]

### 5.2.2 Consumers Also Have an Interest in Inefficiency

Our evaluation of how producers can accumulate market power, either naturally or through politico-legal channels, has so far assumed that the cost of producing additional units of output is insensitive to how large a firm might become.[12] An important, though implicit, consequence of this common analytical approach is that the potential for exploiting market power solely rests with producers. Indeed, assuming that the marginal cost curve is flat also assumes that consumers have no interest in lobbying for anticompetitive prices (since producers who face a common and constant marginal cost would *completely* exit the market if prices did not at least meet that cost). The lowest price at which a market can logically rest in the model we examined above is the competitive price.

---

[8] An interesting but unresolved issue is whether this bidding process fully dissipates the benefits of gaining such legislative favors.

[9] Peltzman's article builds on George Stigler's (1971) pioneering work.

[10] To anticipate our future results, note that "society" encompasses competing interests. Nameless economic performance, as a consequence, tends to lack a special interest.

[11] This type of lobbying is known as "rent seeking", and is socially undesirable not only for the deadweight losses that it directly creates (e.g., the economic opportunities that are lost from exercising market power, as illustrated by area C in Fig. 5.1), but also because producers and political agents must forego potentially more productive opportunities to seek redistributive benefits. Nobel laureate James Buchanan frequently receives credit for bringing these costs to light (e.g., see Mueller 1989, p. 230). Fred McChesney (1987) went even further, highlighting the potential for "political blackmail" to weaken economic performance. In his model, legislative agents not only benefit from creating rents for support constituencies, they also benefit from extracting preexisting private rents. For example, agents may also accept campaign contributions in return for credible promises to forego taxes on accumulated investment.

[12] Notice that the marginal cost curve is flat in Fig. 5.1.

But an important contribution from Chicago School scholars is to have noticed that competition policy tends not to discourage a natural tendency for producers to engage in anticompetitive behavior (i.e., constrain the pricing power of firms that approach a constant marginal cost), but rather facilitates the cartelization of firms that would otherwise face considerable competitive pressures. A normative analysis of competition policy might thus be better served by considering a model where marginal costs eventually increase with output (i.e., the quantity of output that firms are willing to supply increases with prices).

When supply curves slope upward, the floor on feasible prices is no longer the competitive level (as it is when marginal cost is common and constant). Rather, it is the monopsony level, or the infra-competitive price, that maximizes consumer (rather than producer) surplus. In this perhaps more empirically relevant setting, *both* consumers and producers have an incentive to seek regulatory rents. Indeed, just as producers prefer inefficient outcomes that take surplus from consumers, consumers prefer inefficient outcomes that take surplus from producers. Rather than necessarily being a force for efficiency, then, competition policies risk favoring consumers over producers, while weakening economic performance all the same.

Though the danger that consumers pose in this regard is important in principle, it has oftentimes been characterized as having negligible practical importance (e.g., see Baker 2006, p. 485). Evaluated against this backdrop, an ongoing debate about whether competition policy should maximize total or consumer surplus would appear inconsequential.[13] But the evidence developed in Part I of this book moves past the principled argument that consumer surplus standards can put economic performance at risk to robust empirical support that economic performance has significantly suffered in an important sector where the political pressures are unexceptional. In this light, problems of collective action or risks of producer capture that a consumer welfare objective might have productively addressed (e.g., see Neven and Röller 2005 and Baker 2006, respectively) appear to have instead received politically attractive but economically burdensome institutional remedies.[14]

## 5.3 Case Study: Do Consumer Interests Weigh Too Heavily on Insurance Regulation?

We saw in Part I of this book that just as producers can benefit from exploiting bargaining power for private gain (but at the public's expense), so can consumers. We also saw that rather than being an abstract (though theoretically robust) possibility,

[13]Carlton (2007) and Buccirossi (2008) developed introductions to this debate.

[14]This type of normative inference exhibits considerable robustness to modeling assumptions. Economic performance, as evidenced in Part I of this book, appears inferior when evaluated not only in terms of deadweight losses, but also when compared to optimal outcomes in dynamic consistency and real option models. This agreement across intellectually reasonable approaches to antitrust questions suggests that something more than structural concerns for static regressive distributions is necessary to defend consumer surplus standards for competition policy (Falaschetti 2008).

the risk of consumers exploiting political advantage (while damaging economic performance) finds considerable support in data from the US local exchange sector.

Recall too, however, that the telecommunications sector is "special" for its quasi-experimental properties, not because the theories that we evaluated in Part I are particular to this sector. Indeed, Part I implies that electoral/consumer accountability can go too far wherever the potential exists for (i) pressure groups to compete for policy outcomes, (ii) bargaining positions to change as interested parties work their way through a policy's prescriptions, or (iii) market power to allow firms to productively address demand uncertainty.

Given the unremarkable nature of these conditions, we might thus be suspicious about popular claims that other economic sectors are underperforming because producers are too powerful. Could it instead be that too much accountability to consumers is contributing to the realization of inferior outcomes? This section argues, yes!

The deeper message from Part I of this book is that, if too much accountability is problematic when its implications are relatively easy to observe (when economic sectors happen to exhibit attractive experimental properties), then we should be concerned about accountability going too far when politico-legal conditions are ripe, but social consequences are harder to measure. The market for property insurance in catastrophe-prone areas fits this characterization. And though the analytical methods that are used in this section of the book are relatively informal, they continue to yield evidence that pressure for consumer-friendly policies has weakened economic performance.

### *5.3.1 Insurance Can Improve Economic Welfare*

Why would anyone willingly forego considerable sums of money to receive a payoff in the case of an unlikely event? Our question is not about gambling in Vegas but rather about buying insurance. And our answer is that we value money paid for insurance premiums in "good times" less than we do money received for settlements when a catastrophe is realized.

Figure 5.2 illustrates how this observation can make insurance mutually attractive for both buyers and sellers. The first idea that our figure illustrates is that, when it comes to wealth, more is better, but additions to our wealth generate smaller and smaller increases in wellbeing. To see this relationship, consider a wealth increase that would save us from starving and push us over the level of subsistence. Evaluated at this extremely low starting point, the marginal utility of wealth is clearly very large. Indeed, it is the difference between life and death!

But what happens when our wealth increases from, say, \$1 million to \$1.1 million? The increase in wealth is considerable – \$100,000! But would our increase in utility be as great here as it would be if we were escaping subsistence? Probably not.

The concave shape of our utility curve in Fig. 5.2 captures the nature of this relationship. It says that the marginal utility of a dollar is greater when evaluated

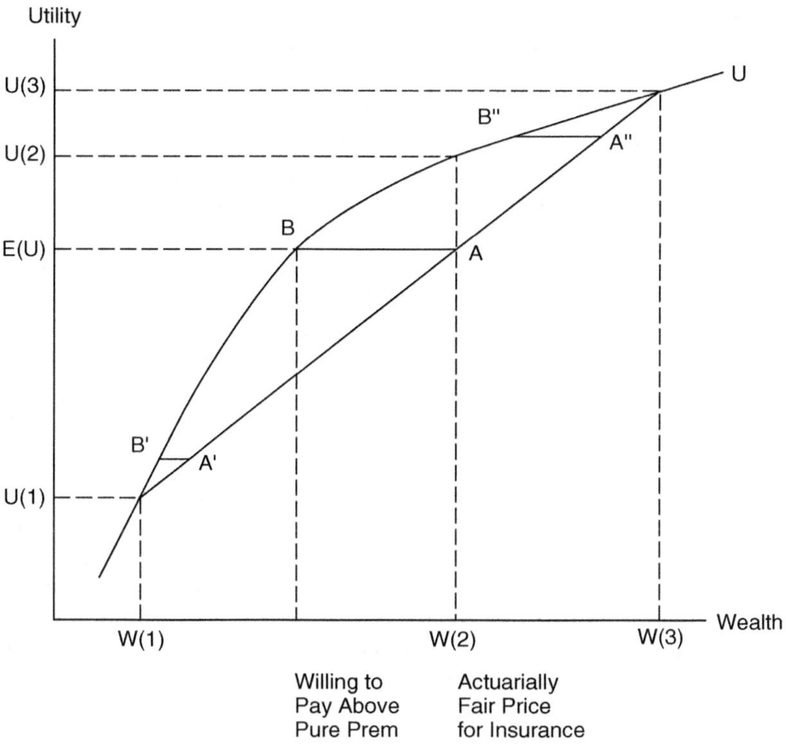


**Fig. 5.2** Decreasing marginal utility of wealth, catastrophic risks, and mutually beneficial trades in the insurance market

at relatively low levels of wealth like $W_1$ than at relatively high levels of wealth like $W_3$.[15]

In this light, assuming that an individual's utility increases with wealth, but at a diminishing rate, appears reasonable. And if individuals can be fairly characterized in this manner, then they will also rationally demand insurance (even at prices that exceed actuarially fair levels). To see why, notice that individuals can reasonably expect a considerable decrease in wealth following a catastrophic event. Given a plausible aversion to risk, then, they can rationally anticipate that benefits from an insurance settlement will exceed costs of premium payments. In other words, risk-averse individuals willingly forego low-valued premium dollars in high-wealth states (when a catastrophe has not been realized) in return for high-valued settlement dollars in low-wealth states (when a catastrophe has been realized).

So far, so good. But to firmly understand how insurance transactions can expand economic opportunities, and how too much political accountability in governing

[15]Note that changing the level of wealth from $W_1$ (where the utility curve is relatively steep) causes a considerably larger change in wellbeing than does changing wealth from $W_3$ (where the utility curve is relatively flat).

those transactions can shrink (rather than facilitate) opportunities, we need to identify combinations of insurance prices and loss probabilities at which insurance is beneficial for demanders *and* suppliers.

Returning to our figure, suppose that a household's wealth without a loss can be represented as $W_3$ while wealth with a loss can be represented as $W_1$. In other words, if a household self-insures and no loss occurs, then it recognizes a relatively high level of utility ($U_3$ in Fig. 5.2). If a loss does occur, then the self-insurer recognizes a relatively low level of utility ($U_1$ in Fig. 5.2).

Given this setup, we can answer the following question – at what prices and loss-probabilities does a rational household buy insurance? To begin addressing this question, let us consider the line segment running from the point ($W_1$, $U_1$) in the southwest portion of the figure to the northeastern point ($W_3$, $U_3$). And note that, for every probability with which a loss can occur (i.e., 0–100%), there exists a point on this segment that represents our household's *expected* utility (i.e., the probability-weighted average of utilities in states where the risk is and is not realized).[16] For example, if a loss occurs with certainty (the probability of a loss equals 100%), then the household's expected utility is $U_1$ (since its wealth will be $W_1$ with certainty). As the probability of a loss decreases, we move northeast along the segment connecting ($W_1$, $U_1$) and ($W_3$, $U_3$), and the utility that a self-insurer realizes *on average* increases accordingly. Ultimately, we must reach the end of this segment ($W_3$, $U_3$) where the household is certain that no loss will occur (the probability of a loss equals zero). Here, our household knows that its wealth will be $W_3$ and can thus fully expect to enjoy a level of utility $U_3$.

Equipped with our representation of expected utilities, we can now identify the conditions under which risk-averse households demand insurance. Suppose that the loss probability is such that the household's expected wealth is $W_2$, and note that a self-insurer's expected utility at this wealth level is E(U) (which, importantly, is less than $U_2$, the *actual* level of utility that realizing the wealth-level $W_2$ with certainty generates). Note further that the "actuarially fair" price for insurance in this case is simply the difference in relevant wealth levels, that is, ($W_3 - W_2$) represents the average claim for which the insurer will be liable.

But no insurance company can simply charge actuarially fair rates – after all, insurers must also pay for operational expenses. Risk-averse households, however, are willing to pay more than the actuarially fair price for insurance – in this case, by an amount up to the difference (A–B). Where does this difference come from? By recognizing that paying anything more would *certainly* leave our household with so little wealth, it could have done better rolling the dice without insurance. In other words, the household's willingness to pay above the actuarially fair price is limited by the level of wealth that makes it indifferent between buying insurance and self-insuring. The highest premium that the household is willing to pay in the present figure, then, is ($W_3 - W_2$) + (A−B), which produces the same level of utility, E(U), as does self-insuring.

[16]Recall that our original "concave" curve relates wealth levels to actual, not expected, utility.

We now have a framework for understanding how insurance markets can facilitate the production of mutual benefits and when laws and regulations instead favor one party at the other's expense. To see this distinction, let us compare the lengths of segments like (A, B), (A′, B′), and (A″, B″) and recall that each segment's length represents the amount that our household is willing to pay for insurance, *above the fair premium*. We should also note that this amount is relatively small for high- and low-probability losses (i.e., the lengths of segments (A′, B′) and (A″, B″) are relatively short). Consequently, evaluated at loss probabilities that correspond to A′ and A″, an insurer's administrative costs are likely to exceed the relatively small excess that households are willing to spend. In cases like these, insurers and households would *both* be better off if households self-insured.

More generally, when risks are low *or* high, market insurance against losses is likely to be inefficient; that is, the insurance transaction is likely to leave at least one party worse off. Consider an extreme where losses are certain. Self-insurance would (implicitly) require premiums that cover only the loss, but market-produced insurance would require a premium that covers the loss and administration costs. Rational households do not demand competitively produced insurance services in cases like this one, or those that approach the symmetric case where losses are certain to not occur.

## 5.3.2 *But Promises Are Hard to Keep*

To develop these insights, we assumed that the costs of transacting are negligible. If we want to understand how political forces tend to move us away from law and economic ideals, however, we should put these costs back into the analysis.

Notice, first, that the above model implicitly assumes that insurance suppliers honestly pay claims. But wouldn't insurers be better off if they could collect premiums before the fact, then deny even legitimate claims afterward? Of course they would!

The problem here is known in the literature as "time inconsistency", a fundamental obstacle to implementing optimal policies that we encountered in both Part I of this book and our Chapter 4 analysis of monetary policy. Modeled consumers from Part I, for example, start by promising to pay local exchange service providers for legitimate costs. They have a strong incentive to renege on this promise, however, after receiving services. Indeed, once telecommunications firms sink capital into producing local exchange services (e.g., loops), the telecoms are willing to supply services at prices that cover only marginal costs. The prospect of being held up in this manner, however, ultimately discourages suppliers from making necessary investments in the first place, and thus weakens economic performance in the longer run. Importantly, this weakness does not come from a lack of technically feasible opportunities but rather from consumers' inability to credibly commit to pay for the full (rather than marginal) cost of local exchange services.

This same problem can plague the insurance sector, but from the opposite direction. Here, demanders and suppliers of insurance services may readily agree that certain premium-coverage combinations make both parties better off. In our Fig. 5.2, such a combination would be one where premiums exceed the actuarially fair level of ($W_3 - W_2$) and fall below the willingness to pay ($W_3 - W_2$) + (A−B), and coverage guarantees a utility level of at least E(U). But in the absence of countervailing forces, the best thing for an insurance company to do, once an insured incurs a loss, is to renege on the promise to pay.

### *5.3.3 Restricting Credit-Based Insurance Scores Can Overly Favor Consumers*

Reputational concerns on behalf of insurance companies can help mitigate this type of ex post opportunism, as can contract law. But recall that laws are the product of public choices and these choices are sensitive to the distributional pressures that interest groups create. Insurance lobbies, for example, may be so powerful that contract law does little to save us from insurers who would opportunistically exploit bargaining advantages.

The potential for opportunistic actions to weaken economic performance also rests with consumers, however, and can be realized when competition policies let consumers hide information about risk assessments (rather than encourage transparent disclosures). Consider, first, the considerable potential for consumers to enjoy better information than do insurers before obtaining coverage. While insurers can collect information from home inspections or health screenings, the information that those investigations produce is likely to be less than what is more readily available to consumers. Consumers may, for example, enjoy years of personal experience with a particular house or have intimate knowledge about symptoms of a hard-to-detect and preexisting health condition. In common cases like these, insurers will not receive a random selection of customers but rather a set of individuals who masquerade as average risks while rationally expecting their insurance benefits to outweigh premium costs.

This propensity for individuals to "adversely select" themselves into transactions is well known as the "lemons problem." To see why, consider the skepticism we often experience when shopping for a used car. Here, sellers can easily enjoy information about an automobile that only firsthand experience would produce – information that can remain hidden to even astute mechanics. In particular, while prospective buyers might know a lot, in general, about the quality of a certain car's make and model, the car's owner likely enjoys additional and hard-to-discover information about the particular car under consideration.

Anticipating this disadvantage, prospective buyers tend to guard themselves by curbing their willingness to pay. They might, for example, be willing to pay only the value of an average-quality car, even if the car being considered appears attractive on the outside. But notice that this skepticism creates a self-fulfilling prophecy – why would a seller let go of a high-quality car if concerns about hidden information discourage buyers from paying a sufficiently high price? In this not so abstract case, only lemons will make their way to the market. Consequently, while trading high-quality cars at high prices might improve the welfare of both buyers and sellers, the prospect of information being strategically shared can preclude the enjoyment of mutual benefits.

Mechanisms that reveal the truth about quality can discourage such inferior outcomes and thus expand opportunities for mutually beneficial trade. Reputable guarantees on used cars, for example, increase confidence that we are not about to buy a lemon. After all, someone who would sell us a lemon has little incentive to accept an enforceable liability to fix problems that are likely to occur.

But while the availability of such mechanisms can strengthen economic performance, the distributional consequences of those mechanisms can be politically formidable. The controversy over "credit scoring" in insurance markets is illustrative.

Insurance companies have found that the credit scores of applicants share a strong and negative correlation with the frequency and level of claims. And a little economic theory suggests that this correlation is more than an artifact – credit scores can reveal salient information that might otherwise remain hidden. Individuals with low credit scores are likely to be "cash constrained" in the sense that their opportunities to consume goods and services are strongly influenced by the amount of cash on hand. Indeed, access to alternative forms of payment (e.g., credit cards) can be prohibitive for individuals with poor credit histories. Economic theory predicts, then, that cash-constrained individuals will look for substitute sources of financial capital, especially in times of emergency.

One such source is an insurance claim, even if it is not legitimate. And to the extent that such implications are more than a theoretical curiosity, insurers have a reasonable interest in their applicants' credit scores. In this case, competition policies that encourage consumers to transparently disclose information can strengthen the insurance market's performance in much the same way that truth-revealing mechanisms about lemons strengthen the car market; that is, by curbing the potential for adverse selection to discourage mutually beneficial transactions.

But are cash-constrained individuals really strategic enough to pursue insurance claims as a source of financial capital? Apparently, they are. Consider the case of Allstate v. Jackson.[17] Following Hurricane Katrina in 2005, Mary Jackson claimed that strong winds caused $16,000 of damage to her home. Allstate, however, did not immediately pay this claim. And while Ms. Jackson was waiting, her house burned down, leading to another claim, this time for $280,000.

These facts, so far, imply that Allstate may have acted in a time-inconsistent manner; that is, collecting premiums up front, then delaying or denying settlements after the fact. Additional evidence suggests, however, that it was Ms. Jackson who strategically used her informational advantage – namely, personal details about

[17] United States District Court, S.D. Alabama, Southern Division. 2008 Indiana Jury Verdict Reporter.

her credit worthiness. At the time of application, Ms. Jackson had previously filed for bankruptcy twice during a 4-month period and made insurance claims for fire-related losses four times over a 10-year period. She was attempting to sell her house when it burned down, and these facts appear to have been unavailable to Allstate when it wrote Ms. Jackson's policy.

A jury thus concluded that Ms. Jackson's claims were motivated by financial distress, not legitimate losses. In terms of our adverse selection theory, prospective insurance clients like Ms. Jackson can be characterized as lemons. Suppliers of insurance services, like demanders of automobiles, want to avoid lemons. But to the extent that insurers cannot distinguish lemons from non-lemons up front, they will instead demand higher premiums from everyone to compensate for individuals who strategically hide information about their likelihood to file claims. And if too many non-lemons balk at these inflated premiums (because self-insuring is more economical than cross-subsidizing individuals who strategically hide their risks), then the best response for insurers may be to exit the market altogether.[18]

An efficiency-enhancing role for competition policy would thus seem to be one of encouraging more transparent disclosures from consumers. But while such laws might improve economic performance in general, they could have negative distributional consequences for individuals who benefit from keeping their high-risk status a secret. And restricting insurers from using credit scores to inform underwriting decisions may very well serve this distributional interest rather than the greater good that can come from strong economic performance.

The theory and illustration developed here suggest that restricting insurers from using credit information benefits a concentrated few people like Ms. Jackson, but forecloses mutually beneficial trades more generally as insurers attempt to protect themselves through tentative coverage and pricing strategies. Even more, such restrictions do little to address the deeper problem - a considerable number of people who reside in an unusually wealthy nation face such tight cash-constraints that filing illegitimate insurance claims appears attractive. Nevertheless, 48 states restrict credit scoring, and consumer advocates and state regulators are pressuring lawmakers to further constrain this practice (Karlinsky and Fidei 2008).[19]

### *5.3.4 Regulation Through Litigation Can Overly Favor Consumers*

Restrictions on credit-based insurance scoring can let individuals strategically act on private information, tilting distributions in favor of consumers while creating a lemons problem that weakens insurance markets more generally. The potential for

---

[18]In a case like this, the market will consist of households that have a high probability of filing a claim. Recall from our Fig. 5.2 that insurance contracts are unlikely to be written for extremely high and low risks.

[19]Florida's Office of Insurance Regulation (OIR), for example, is considering (as of this writing) a proposal "to ensure that rates or premiums associated with credit reports or scores are not unfairly discriminatory" (Coldny et al. 2008b).

consumers to exploit bargaining advantages, however, is not isolated to the time period before a loss occurs. Rather, opportunistic actions that are available to consumers after a loss also weaken economic performance. Moreover, just as competition policies have sometimes overly served consumers' distributional objectives before insurance contracts are written, they can also favor consumers too strongly by allowing for an opportunistic expansion of coverage after even legitimate losses.

This problem is sometimes referred to as "regulation through litigation."[20] As we saw earlier, insurers have an incentive to opportunistically deny claims after the fact. Reputational concerns and the law can productively address this problem by facilitating low-cost and durable commitments to fulfill agreed-upon obligations. To be sure, the law can stop short of what is ideal on this dimension. But it can also go too far by expanding coverage beyond the bounds of original agreements.

Expansions like these benefit affected consumers (at least after the fact) as well as politicians who might cater to such opportunism in return for increased support. Pursuing such distributional objectives, however, can weaken economic performance more generally, as premiums must increase to pay not only covered losses but also those that fall outside the scope of original contracts. These price increases discourage mutually beneficial trades by creating a wedge between what non-opportunistic customers are willing to pay and the price that insurers must charge to take on the politico-legal risk that liabilities will ultimately exceed agreed-upon coverage. Even more, to the extent that consumers' ability to opportunistically expand coverage can stay one step ahead of insurers' ability to price those expansions, insurers may find it best to completely exit from the market.

A 2004 Florida court decision illustrates how competition policy can evolve to overly favor consumers through this channel, shifting the burden of paying for non-covered flood damages to insurers who originally agreed to cover only wind-related losses.[21] In short, this decision required insurance companies to fully pay up to a policy's limits, even when the peril that was covered under these limits (in this case, wind damage) only partially contributed to the total loss (in this case, wind and flood damage). Florida subsequently experienced abnormally active hurricane seasons, and insurers found themselves settling claims for the full limits of wind policies, even though much of the destruction was attributed to flooding (Karlinsky and Abate 2008).

Florida's Supreme Court reversed this decision in 2007. However, the fundamental political pressures for inefficient regulation through litigation still exist, and not only in Florida. As the introduction to this book documents, for example, claims of this nature continue to be litigated in Mississippi.

Finally, it is interesting to note that this type of problem is unlikely due to the ignorance of either the relevant government agents or their constituents. Following Hurricane Katrina, for example, a number of CEOs from large insurance companies met with the White House's Chairman of Gulf Coast Reconstruction, Donald

---

[20] See, for example, Abraham (2002).

[21] Mierzwa v. Florida Windstorm Underwriting Association, 877 So.2d 774 (Fla. 4th DCA 2004).

Powell.[22] For policymakers, the meeting's objective was to better understand why, almost a year after the storm, insurers were still reluctant to do business in the devastated region. To this point, one CEO observed, "Mr. Chairman, we're not coming back for any price."

This statement fits with our model where "exit" becomes optimal when an interested party's "voice" has too little force. In the pressure-group model that we have been using to rationalize various politico-legal and law-and-economic phenomena, producers exercise market power by curbing output so that prices can be raised above their competitive level. But in this episode, raising prices to *any* level does not appear to be enough for insurers to maintain a sufficient presence in risk-prone areas. The CEO's comment is more consistent with the prospect of political agents receiving so much pressure after a disaster that policy commitments to prices and other contractual obligations have a small chance of being upheld.

Kenneth Abraham (2007, p. 180) independently arrived at a similar conclusion, noting that "Harsh legal treatment (or the prospect of it)... undoubtedly exacerbated insurers' reluctance to continue writing coverage on coastal property". To be sure, insurers certainly have an incentive to strategically deny claims. But if their market power let them get away with making profits in this manner, they would want to enter, not exit, the market. Evidence of exit, instead, is more consistent with consumers not being able to credibly promise against opportunistically expanding contracts after the fact.

The repetition of experiences like these suggests that the root cause is a durable one. Neither consumers nor producers have a special interest in economic efficiency (and thus neither do politicians). To do better, then, we may need stable institutions to strike a more productive balance in pressures that producers and consumers bring to such matters. And to the extent that public laws and organizations are unable to reach this ideal, lawyers and business managers may have an interest in taking matters into their own hands, developing non-market strategies that mitigate the omnipresent political risks to productive economic activity. We will return to these types of strategies at the end of this chapter.

### *5.3.5 Rate Regulation Can Facilitate Consumer Monopsonies Instead of Checking Producer Monopolies*

Price controls have long served political goals at the expense of economic performance,[23] and the regulation of insurance premiums appears to follow this history. Except for Illinois, every US state controls some aspect of pricing insurance products (Royce 2008). But social science offers little in the way of an efficiency rationale. And consistent with this lack of theoretical support, jurisdictions where rate

[22] This example draws on personal experiences of the author in 2006, during his service as a senior economist for the President's Council of Economic Advisers.

[23] Thomas Sowell (2007) developed an accessible review of this history.

regulation is missing appear to perform at least as well as their regulated counterparts (Tennyson 2007).

In considerable part, this difference between competition policies that we observe and those that would better serve economic performance can reasonably be attributed to the political pressures that we have studied throughout this book – pressures that can encourage regulators to favor inefficient distributions over more widely spread opportunities. Motivation for early insurance controls came, at least superficially, from a concern that competitive pressures would cause an *underpricing* of risk and thus destabilize the market for insurance. Over time, however, that concern appears to have waned, and an emphasis on preventing excessive rates has became more prevalent. This emphasis is especially strong in the political pursuit of keeping insurance "affordable" for high-risk, vulnerable constituents. Over two-thirds of US states, for example, publicly operate "residual markets" that subsidize premiums for risk-prone homeowners (Tennyson 2007, pp. 6–7).

While catering to politically attractive support constituencies, however, these controls can create considerable economic damage. To the extent that controls push prices below their competitive levels, for example, the quantity of coverage that insurers willingly supply decreases. And the publicly supported residual markets that often respond to such exits fuel households' incentives to accept too much risk and file illegitimate claims, as a political calculus of "who receives what from whom" replaces economic costs and benefits to allocate a shrinking quantity of insurance services.[24]

The consistency with which these theoretical implications find empirical support led Tennyson (2007) to conclude that the damage to economic performance from overly favoring consumer interests eventually becomes too heavy to sustain.[25] Politico-legal processes, nevertheless, appear prone to inefficiently serving those interests. The case of Florida is, again, illustrative.

Of the 10 most costly US hurricanes (in terms of insured property losses through 2007), only 1 missed Florida (Insurance Information Institute).[26] Moreover, as of 2007, Florida leads the United States with almost $2.5 trillion of insured coastal

[24]Tennyson (2007) reviewed the literature on these theoretical implications and supporting evidence. Despite this scientific backing to the contrary, however, regulatory officials continually describe such controls as "experiments" whose prospects for success are realistic. In doing so, they even take the logically inconsistent stance that stringent controls are necessary to achieve a "free market" (see, e.g., Bushouse 2007). To be sure, satisfying the institutional pre-conditions for markets to perform well is not trivial – but the careful inquiries reviewed here agree that common controls on the insurance sector have failed on this margin. This disconnect may speak less to the ignorance of associated political officials than to the unyielding nature of distributive pressures that fundamentally govern social choices.

[25]Tennyson (2007, p. 19) observed, for example, that "(r)egulations cannot eradicate the underlying incentive forces that govern decisions in markets, and regulations that ignore these forces lead to unintended consequences that worsen market outcomes."

[26]In 1989, the sixth most costly hurricane, Hugo, struck the US mainland in Georgia and moved northward through South Carolina, North Carolina, and Virginia (Insurance Information Institute).

property (Insurance Information Institute),[27] and many climate forecasts see more turbulent weather patterns ahead.[28] An already large exposure for Florida insurers may thus be growing.

In this light, the risk of loss to existing Florida properties appears to be high and may be increasing. Our model of insurance demand (illustrated in Fig. 5.2), then, implies that the room for insurers and property owners to mutually benefit from trading exposures to catastrophic risks is small and may be narrowing. Forces for actuarially sound premium increases may thus be growing stronger, but if the range of mutually beneficial prices is simultaneously decreasing, demands for political action may be growing too (even if those solutions are inefficient).

Recent Florida history is consistent with just such a story. In 2002, the Florida state legislature created Citizens Property Insurance Corporation to provide a "safety net" for "Floridians without private insurance options."[29] Private options may have disappeared, however, for legitimate reasons, that is, because rate regulations did not respect the previously described economic fundamentals. But rather than address this possibility, the governor and almost every state legislator may have aggravated it, agreeing in January 2007 to expand Citizens' ability to underwrite coverage and drastically reduce the premiums that it can charge (Kleindienst and Bushouse 2007).

Citizens thus became an even more attractive substitute for private producers of insurance services, who also directly received pressure from the 2007 legislation and subsequent actions by Florida's Office of Insurance Regulation (OIR) to reduce rates. But consistent with the lack of "private options" noted above, the rates that private insurers were able to charge at the time may have already been too low. Bruce Douglas (former Chair of Citizens) observed, for example, that Florida's premium regulations had already created a highly distorted rate structure.[30]

Faced with apparently intensifying political pressures for even lower rates, large private insurers have now stopped supplying property insurance to any new customers and are refusing to renew policies for existing customers (Garcia 2008b). This pattern of political pressure for lower prices leading to an exodus of suppliers is consistent with our Part I model of how regulation can cartelize consumers at the expense of economic performance more generally. That model also rationalizes other damaging consequences of what may be too much consumer influence in the Florida insurance market, such as an increased rationing of insurance services through non-price mechanisms (e.g., delaying the servicing of claims) and attempts

---

[27] New York is a close second, and Texas a distant third with less than 40 percent of either Florida's or New York's value (Insurance Information Institute).

[28] See, for example, Risk Management Solutions (2006).

[29] Citizens Property Insurance Corporation.

[30] Mr. Douglas observed that, "when we got storms in 2004–2005, people accustomed to paying a $600 premium faced a $2,000 premium and they went ballistic. But $600 wasn't even close to a realistic rate" (Zucco 2008).

to keep the benefits of anticompetitive pricing in state while exporting the costs to more diffuse political constituents.[31]

## 5.4 Tail Risks and Term Limits

Term limits can appear to be an attractive mechanism for aligning political interests with those of consumer electorates. But term limits also shorten a politician's planning horizon and can thus give rise to regulations that put economic performance at risk. Rather than pursuing a fundamentally sound plan for regulating the insurance sector, for example, term-limited politicians may favor undercapitalized insurers. Doing so weakens performance in the long run, but can favor consumers enough in the short run to be politically attractive.

To see the roots of this problem, we need to understand the motivation for financial services firms (like insurance companies) to take on too much "tail risk" - a small probability of incurring a large loss. We can then build up to a rationalization of why overly accountable political agents might favor such firms, rather than pursue a more productive policy on insurance competition.

Financial service firms are regularly evaluated against some benchmark. We might compare returns from a mutual fund against the performance of an index of stocks, for example, to gauge the performance of a fund's managers. In doing so, we gain a metric for disciplining managers to act in our best interest.

However, such disciplinary devices also create perverse incentives for financial service providers. To be sure, these providers can outperform a benchmark by exercising an unusually high level of skill. But they can also do so by pursuing risks that fall outside of the benchmark's scope. In this latter case, managers will appear to achieve a superior level of performance, since their high level of hidden risk tends to generate greater returns than does the lower risk benchmark. This excess reward has less to do with skill, however, than with lemons masquerading as experts by taking hard-to-see risks.

Moreover, these opportunistic managers can appear to outperform their benchmarks for considerable lengths of time. They do so not by indiscriminately taking risks but rather by carefully taking on "tail risk." Tail risk refers to a strategy where financial managers expose themselves to small chances of incurring large losses. Most of the time, this strategy lets managers appear to outperform the market, since the risk will infrequently be realized while the reward for risk-taking can be paid more reliably.

Over short time-horizons, then, consumers will enjoy relatively high returns, but not high enough to compensate for the hidden risks that financial managers are

[31] Former Chairman Douglas also explained how insufficient premium revenue may have led to Citizens' inadequate capacity to service claims (Zucco 2008). Winans (2008) reviewed the pattern of cross-subsidization that may ultimately see voters in low risk states rescuing undercapitalized public providers like Citizens.

taking. Rather, a disproportionate share of the reward for hidden risks will tend to fall to the managers. As in any other principal–agent setting, managerial agents want to enjoy the benefits of "shirking" while passing the cost onto their principals. In this case, the benefit is increased compensation from the appearance of above-average performance, and the cost is the difference in returns between what investors would have received in a competitive environment in which tail risks are transparent and what they actually receive when managers can privately benefit from information advantages.

Evaluations over longer time-horizons, on the other hand, let us better distinguish performance based on skill from performance that superficially appears to come from skill, but really comes from opportunistic risk-taking. Insurance companies with long track records, for example, are less likely to have used tail-risk strategies to drive their performance than are young start-ups. Both the start-up and established firms want to attract capital and premiums. The start-ups, however, are not as certain that they will be around for the long haul and can thus have shorter planning horizons than do more established firms. This shorter horizon, in turn, makes tail-risk strategies more attractive; that is, the large losses associated with these risks (but not the considerable benefits) have a relatively small chance of being realized during the shortened planning period.

One way to take on such risks is to maintain a smaller capital stake in financial operations than is socially optimal. In normal times, this strategy allows insurers to charge low premiums while maintaining a sufficient cushion for paying claims. When the small chance of a catastrophic event is finally realized, however, insurers who once looked like stellar performers (i.e., providing ample coverage for low premiums) will be revealed as tail-risk lemons.

These tail-risk takers can flourish when competition policies overly favor consumers. To see why, notice that purchasers of property insurance have little incentive to evaluate the integrity of their insurers, since considerable public protection exists against an insurer experiencing weakness.[32] The task of prudently monitoring insurance companies thus gets passed to state insurance regulators.

However, these regulators can become so accountable to consumers that they not only have a weak incentive to productively oversee insurers but also have a strong incentive to pursue distributive rents at the expense of long-term economic performance. To start, recall our earlier discussion about insurance rate-regulation, and notice that as pressure from consumers to reduce rates increases, so must the propensity for strongly capitalized insurers to exit the market (since even prudent capital levels must be excluded from the rate base when regulations force premiums too low). We might hope that regulators would resist this pressure, given the strong chance that undercapitalized firms will, sooner or later, encounter considerable difficulty in paying claims for the most demanding perils. Instead, regulators

---

[32]Florida, for example, provides such protections through the Florida Insurance Guaranty Association. Depositors, likewise, tend not to be careful monitors, since public deposit insurance provides a backstop for weaknesses that banks might encounter.

can face strong democratic pressures to favor the tail-risk takers, and this incentive is especially strong when relevant politicians face term limits.[33]

Term limits are frequently characterized as increasing the accountability of political agents to consumer electorates. However, limits can also encourage politicians to accept too much tail risk on behalf of their electoral principals. Term limits create a relatively short time-horizon for politicians, during which (i) the tail risks are unlikely to be realized and (ii) political credit is available for those who provide insurance at a low premium cost. And while the lucky politician will appear to perform well as long as the tail risk goes unrealized, consumers bear the eventual burden of an insurance sector that cannot productively respond to a low-chance/high-cost catastrophe.

This perfect storm may be brewing in Florida, where important policymakers face tight term limits. Coincident with episodes of "regulation by litigation" and of tightening rate regulation described above, large underwriters have been trimming exposure to Florida's property insurance market.[34] The state thus created a subsidized firm in 2002, Citizens Property Insurance Corporation, to *temporarily* act as an "insurer of last resort". Citizens is now Florida's largest insurer of homes, condominiums, and apartments (Garcia 2008c).

Faced with an increasing cost of subsidization,[35] however, Citizens also appears to be getting cold feet. "Domestic companies" are thus being encouraged to facilitate a "takeout process" that transfers policies from Citizens to private insurers at rates below those charged by Citizens (Garcia 2008a, 2008c).[36] Domestics are incorporated under Florida law and now hold over a 30% share of Florida's property insurance market (Vogel 2008).

Consistent with the theory of tail-risk strategies outlined above, these relatively young companies appear to be considerably undercapitalized (Vogel 2008).[37] For example, while senior government officials have publicly characterized domestics as able to withstand a 1-in-250-year storm, the over-century-old insurance-rating firm, A.M. Best, has only rated *one* of Florida's domestics. And that one earned a "financial strength rating" of C (weak)! (Hemenway 2008).

Tennyson (2007, p. 14) explained how this type of disconnect can emerge from domestics naturally enjoying a comparative regulatory advantage. Such an

---

[33]"Relevant politicians" not only include the regulators themselves, but also those who nominate, approve, and oversee the regulators.

[34]See, for example, Garcia (2008a, 2008b).

[35]By Order No. 87822-06, for example, Florida's Office of Insurance Regulation (OIR) approved a new assessment of 1.4% on premiums paid for all new policies and policy renewals through Citizens, starting December 15, 2008 (Colodny et al. 2008 (September 4)). And by statute, a catastrophic storm would allow this assessment to increase to *45 percent* for customers of Citizens, while exposing those insured with companies other than Citizens (even those with auto insurance policies) to upwards of a six percent assessment (Garcia 2008a, c).

[36]In 2006, Florida offered $250 million in matching loans to encourage the development of a domestic market (Vogel 2008).

[37]Domestics tend to be less than ten years old (Vogel 2008).

advantage plausibly grows from domestics having a more captive in-state support constituency than do carriers writing policies across the States. In this light, it is unsurprising that domestics appear to receive favorable treatment and, despite posing risks to economic performance, earn considerable praise from senior political officials (see, e.g., Bushouse 2007 and Hemenway 2008).

Inefficiently low premiums and a weak capital base are anything but a recipe for economic success.[38] Nevertheless, encouraged by term-limited office holders, state-backed domestics (and even Citizens itself) appear to be following a politically attractive but economically destructive tail-risk strategy. Political support for this type of strategy (e.g., through Government-Sponsored Enterprises (GSEs)) may have played an important role in the international financial market crisis of 2008. Indeed, influential politicians like US Representative Barney Frank (D-MA) appear to have explicitly acknowledged their appetite for tail-risk strategies, declaring that

> I do not want the same kind of focus on safety and soundness... I want to roll the dice a little bit more in this situation towards subsidized housing. (*Wall Street Journal*)

The cases reviewed here suggest that Florida and other states are building their insurance sectors on a similarly weak political foundation.

## 5.5 How Big Is This Problem?

Part I of this book, as well as the last several subsections, highlights how competition policies that listen too much to consumers can weaken economic performance, and may have done so in the telecommunications and insurance sectors. The question to which we now turn is whether this source of politico-legal risk is isolated or can be expected to have a broad reach.

One way to address this question is to investigate even more sectors for evidence of too much consumer accountability. But since a selective search could produce confirming evidence, doing so may not be very persuasive. Instead, we may learn more about the prospect for too much accountability by considering a sector that should not matter for regulators who are more interested in promoting economic efficiency than facilitating political distributions.

This strategy builds on the insight that an optimal level of policing does not catch every crime. An optimal level of enforcing competition policies, likewise, does not extinguish every possibility of anticompetitive behavior. Rather, it productively allows for behavior where the social cost of detection, prosecution, etc. is too high.

To the extent that we observe inconsequential cases being investigated, then, we can more confidently infer that competition policy really can become too accountable, and the negative consequences for economic performance can be more widespread than we can document in this book. Consider, for example, the

---

[38] A qualitatively identical combination characterized the S&L industry before its catastrophe in the 1980s, and characterizes plan sponsors of defined benefit retirement plans today (see, for example, Falaschetti and Orlando (2008, Chapter 14)).

$1.8 billion market for packaged ice, which is (as of this writing) under investigation for anticompetitive activity. To be sure, this market appears large relative to standards by which individuals judge their own welfare. But $1.8 billion accounts for just over *one-one hundredth of a percent* of the US economy's almost $14 trillion activity, and any technology gains that are made in this sector appear unlikely to spill over to other areas of the economy in an important way.

Even more, allegations are not that the entire $1.8 billion sector is collusive. Rather, the main suspect appears to be a company that allegedly conspired to suppress competition in Detroit, Michigan (Wilke 2008). But Michigan's average temperature is 46.0°F (measured in the relatively hot year of 2007).[39] And the largest ice manufacturers do not appear to be marketing toward industrial applications, which might otherwise point to average temperatures and ice demand being largely unrelated. Rather, partygoers appear to be the target audience (Wilke 2008).[40]

These casual observations further the difficulty that we already encountered when trying to rationalize competition policy as regularly checking producers' abusive accumulations of market power. If competition policy really tends to have an efficiency goal, then why do its enforcers appear ready to serve distributional interests in an inconsequential sector?

## 5.6 Governance Opportunities

We started this chapter, and have now begun to end it, with several discouraging observations. Prosperous societies are a recent phenomenon and, even now, are not the norm. This fact pattern is unlikely to have come from a lack of appreciation for advances in social science, however. Indeed, while a scientific understanding of policy principles is only an accessible textbook away, a very large number of people continue to experience lives that are "nasty, brutish, and short."

To the extent that preferences for peace and prosperity are common, then, there must exist resistant social forces working against us. We have uncovered a source of persistence here – neither producers nor consumers have a *dominant* interest in efficiency (and thus neither do governing politicians). Robust theoretical models suggest that these individuals can be more interested in distributions that favor themselves than expansions of economic opportunities. And since laws that give structure to even the freest of markets are strongly influenced by these political forces, we should not be surprised when rules that govern economic exchange cartelize interested producers and consumers rather than ease the frictions that discourage mutually beneficial trades.

---

[39]This average is closer to that of the coldest state in the US (Maine, 40.6 degrees) than the hottest (Florida 71.6 degrees). Source: NOAA, http://climvis.ncdc.noaa.gov/cgi-bin/cag3/state-map-display.pl, accessed August 6, 2008.

[40]The jingle for the largest ice-maker, for example, is "Good times are in the Bag!" (Wilke 2008). Sadly for Detroit, however, good times have really been in the bag, with population and economic performance declining for almost 60 years (Glaeser and Gyourko 2005).

Unfortunately, there is no "invisible hand" theorem, suggesting that this condition is an aberration and that political processes tend to generate socially attractive laws. Rather than hopelessly condemn societies to poor performance, however, this insight highlights a constrained but considerable set of opportunities for individuals working at the intersection of politics, law, and business to improve social welfare. The remainder of this chapter discusses a handful of such strategies.

### *5.6.1 What Can Politics Do Better?*

Competition policy aims to curb inefficient restraints on trade, with an explicit concern about the potential for and realization of monopoly. To the extent that power naturally concentrates on an economy's supply side, this focus on consumer welfare may be well placed. In particular, by attempting to maximize consumer surplus in a world that otherwise favors producers, antitrust law and related regulations would, coincidentally, do well at expanding economic opportunities in general.

This rationalization receives considerable support from both academic and popular media, in part because experts have seen little risk of consumers opportunistically benefiting from competition policy (Baker 2003, 2006). The formal evidence developed in Part I of this book, however, strongly argues against such a confident conclusion. Not only do the empirical correlations on which this evidence builds exhibit considerable robustness, but the economic models that help us interpret those correlations exhibit remarkable agreement, suggesting that the risk of too much consumer influence exists not only in the important telecommunications sector but also in any sector whose governance is subject to pressure-group competition and policy credibility. The fact that this risk appears to have been realized in other important sectors, such as insurance, may thus be unsurprising.

Taken as a whole, then, the evidence that this book brings together may offer a stronger case for holding competition policy to a *total* welfare standard. But even if this policy prescription is correct, simply highlighting the prospect of improved economic performance is not enough to see it implemented. Rather, any move in this direction must overcome politically powerful interests, which may lie with consumers and electorates in this case.

Institutional reforms that insulate regulators from these distributional interests offer a durable, but difficult-to-implement, strategy for achieving this objective. In particular, competition policy might improve from moving deliberations to an environment where policymakers are less susceptible to capture from producers *and* consumers. The evidence developed and reviewed here suggests that revisiting popular democratic governance features, such as electing regulators, limiting campaign contributions, and term-limiting office holders, may help. Moreover, success with similarly structured deliberations over monetary policy (reviewed in Chapter 4 of this book) suggests that such undemocratic processes can indeed deliver both a heightened level and broader distribution of economic opportunities.

### 5.6.2 What Can the Law Do Better?

More immediate improvement opportunities may be available to lawyers. Supreme Court Justice Antonin Scalia and others have argued that judges are persuaded not by what is best for the case at hand but by whether a resolution of the case at hand will also productively guide future deliberations (Scalia and Garner 2008). By this standard, a "good" argument cannot point to distributional consequences as evidence of its quality. Indeed, because preferences over distributions can be sensitive to context, distributional concerns tend to provide inconsistent guidance for future decisions.

A more attractive argument, instead, is one that reasonably leads to an expansion of opportunities so that, over time, laws and regulations broadly raise living standards rather than simply redistribute resources. Understanding how consumers (as well as producers) can favor distributional advantages over efficiency gains can help lawyers succeed in developing this type of argument. And while this strategy can be personally rewarding for lawyers, it can also help push competition policy onto a superior evolutionary path.

### 5.6.3 What Can Business Do Better?

Business managers may find themselves similarly situated; that is, able to employ non-market strategies that not only improve their own organizations' performance but also expand economic opportunities more generally. Rather than taking a traditional approach to lobbying political agents with information about a policy's unintended consequences, for example, businesses may also want to become political entrepreneurs themselves. An attractive strategy here, both privately and publicly, can be one of organizing otherwise diffuse individuals who tend to enjoy rents from a business's activities.

Energy companies appear to have recently bolstered such efforts, advertising through popular outlets that a windfall profits tax could weaken retirement security. They have essentially argued that "we're all energy companies now", as individual pension and retirement savings heavily depend on the energy sector's performance. The distributional winners from a windfall profits tax are relatively easy to identify and have so far appeared to generate considerable support for just such a tax. To the extent that such a redistribution would weaken economic performance, however, the energy companies' self-interested organizational efforts may help create a larger set of opportunities that can be enjoyed more widely.

Even more, managers might extend models like those developed and reviewed throughout this book to formally measure and productively anticipate the business cost of common politico-legal risks. Fundamentally, these risks depend on how well insulated are policy and legal deliberations from distributional pressures and can thus predictably vary across businesses that operate under different institutional frameworks. They can also predictably vary for the same business across time, as the distribution of bargaining power between interests evolves in measurable ways.

Quantifying these risks can improve the productivity not only of non-market-lobbying/organizing strategies but also of product and service development decisions. Indeed, while these types of decisions frequently consider legal and economic risks, they often ignore how politics interacts with law and economics. And while taking a more systemic view of competitive landscapes in this manner can produce private benefits, it can also create widespread benefits by bringing more productive forces to bear on politico-legal processes.

## References

Abraham, Kenneth S. (2002). The insurance effects of regulation by litigation. In W. Kip Viscusi (Ed.), *Regulation through litigation* (pp. 212–243). Washington, DC: AEI Press.

Abraham, Kenneth S. (2007). The hurricane Katrina insurance claims. *Virginia Law Review (In Brief)*, 93(August), 173–180.

Acemoglu, Daron (2002). Why not a political Coase Theorem? social conflict, commitment and politics. Working paper, MIT Department of Economics.

Acemoglu, Daron (2003). The form of property rights: oligarchic vs. democratic societies. NBER Working Paper 10037 (October).

Acemoglu, Daron, Simon Johnson, and James A. Robinson (2001). The colonial origins of comparative development: and empirical investigation. *American Economic Review* 91(5), 1369–1401.

Baker, Jonathan (2003). The case for antitrust enforcement. *Journal of Economic Perspectives* 17(4), 27–50.

Baker, Jonathan (2006). Competition policy as a political bargain. *Antitrust Law Journal* 73(2), 483–530.

Buccirossi, Paolo (2008). Introduction. In Paolo Buccirossi (ed.) *Handbook of Antitrust*. Cambridge and London: MIT Press.

Bushouse, Kathy (2007). Q&A with insurance commissioner Kevin McCarty. *Orlando Sentinel*, October 21. orlandosentinel.com/business/insurance/sfl-1021mccartyqa,0,6368803.story. Accessed 12 October 2008.

Carlton, Dennis (2007). Does antitrust need to be modernized? *Journal of Economic Perspectives* 21(3), 155–176.

Citizens Property Insurance Corporation. https://www.citizensfla.com/. Accessed 19 October 2008.

Coase, Ronald (1960). The problem of social cost. *Journal of Law and Economics* 1(October), 1–44.

Colodny, Fass, Talenfeld, Karlinsky, and Abate (2008). OIR approves Citizens' 1.4% emergency assessment fee. *Florida Insurance Bulletin* September 4.

Coldny, Fass, Talenfeld, Karlinsky, and Abate (2008b). Insurance consumer advocate proposes amendment to credit score rule. *Florida Insurance Bulletin*, October 27.

Falaschetti, Dino (2008). Can lobbying prevent anticompetitive outcomes? Evidence on consumer monopsony in telecommunications. *Journal of Competition Law and Economics*, Advance Access published on June 4, 2008, doi:10.1093/joclec/nhn014.

Falaschetti, Dino, and Michael J. Orlando (2008). *Money, Financial Intermediation, and Governance*. Gloucestershire: Edward Elgar Publishing.

Friedman, David D. (2000). *Law's Order: What Economics Has to Do with Law and Why It Matters*. Princeton and Oxford: Princeton University Press.

Galor, Oded (2005). The transition from stagnation to growth: unified growth theory. In P. Aghion and S. Durlauf (Eds.), *Handbook of economic growth* (pp. 171–293). Amsterdam: North-Holland.

Garcia, Beatrice E. (2008a). Local insurers writing policies, but avoiding some areas. *Miami Herald*, May 28. http://www.miamiherald.com/home/v-print/story/546932.htm. Accessed 28 May 2008.

Garcia, Beatrice E. (2008b). Insurer: no new policies, agents. *Miami Herald*, July 12. http://www.miamiherald.com/business/v-print/story/602191.html. Accessed 16 July 2008.

Garcia, Beatrice E. (2008c). How secure is Citizens Property Insurance? *Miami Herald*, July 14. http://www.miamiherald.com/business_monday/v-print/story/603228.html. Accessed 16 July 2008.

Glaeser, Edward L. and Joseph Gyourko (2005). Urban decline and durable housing. *Journal of Political Economy* 113(2), 345–375.

Hemenway, Chad (2008). Florida regulators, Citizens Property Insurance Corp. defend take-out process. *BestWire*, November 11. http://www.bestwire.com/. Accessed 12 November 2008.

Insurance Information Institute. http://www.iii.org/media/facts/statsbyissue/hurricanes/. Accessed 19 October 2008.

Karlinsky, Fred E. and Maria E. Abate (2008). Putting a stop to the parade of horribles. *FORC Journal* 19(1), 27–30

Karlinsky, Fred E. and Richard J. Fidei (2008). Credit-based insurance scores. *FORC Journal* 19(1), 30–32.

Kleindienst, Linda and Kathy Bushouse (2007). Florida legislature passes bill to lower insurance rates. *South Florida Sun-Sentinel*, January 23.

McChesney, Fred S. (1987). Rent extraction and rent creation in the economic theory of regulation. *Journal of Legal Studies* 16(1), 101–118.

Mueller, Dennis C. (1989). *Public choice II*. Cambridge, New York, and Melbourne: Cambridge University Press.

Neven, Damien and Lars-Hendrik Röller (2005). Consumer surplus vs. welfare standard in a political economy model of merger control. *International Journal of Industrial Organization* 23(9–10), 665–668.

Peltzman, Sam (1976). Toward a more general theory of regulation. *Journal of Law & Economics* 19(2), 211–240.

Rajan, Raghuram G. and Luigi Zingales (2003). *Saving Capitalism from the Capitalists: Unleashing the Power of Financial Markets to Create Wealth and Spread Opportunity*. New York: Crown Business.

Risk Management Solutions (2006). http://www.rms.com/newspress/PR_2006_0323_HUActivityRates.asp. Accessed 19 October 2008

Royce, Ed (2008). The forgotten financial sector. *Wall Street Journal*, April 16, A18.

Scalia, Antonin and Bryan A. Garner (2008). *Making your case: the art of persuading judges*. St. Paul, Minnesota: Thomson/West.

Sowell, Thomas (2007). *Basic Economics: a Common Sense Guide to the Economy*, 3rd edition. Tennessee: Basic Books.

Stigler, George J. (1971). The theory of economic regulation. *Bell Journal of Economics and Management Science* 2(1), 3–21.

Tennyson, Sharon (2007). Efficiency consequences of rate regulation in insurance markets. *Networks Financial Institute Policy Brief*, 2007-PB-03.

Vogel, Mike (2008). A game of risk for small insurers. *FloridaTrend.com – The Website of Florida Business*. June 1.

*Wall Street Journal* (2008) Opinion: what they said about Fan and Fred. October 2. http://online.wsj.com/article/SB122290574391296381.html. Accessed 15 November 2008.

Weil, David (2004). *Economic growth*. Boston: Addison Wesley.
Wilke, John R. (2008). Collusion inquiry targets ice companies. *Wall Street Journal*, August 7, B1.
Winans, Brent (2008). Florida flirting with hurricane insurance disaster. *IRMI Insights*, August. http://www.irmi.com/Insights/Articles/2008/Winans-Citizens-Hurricane-CAT-Fund.pdf. Accessed 19 October 2008.
Zucco, Tom (2008). Douglas leaves Citizens more stable. *St. Petersburg Times*, July 25. http://www.tampabay.com/news/business/banking/article739384.ece. Accessed 28 July 2008.

# Chapter 6
# Business

## Shareholder Accountability and Corporate Governance

Corporations should serve shareholders' interests – they "own" the firms, after all. But judging from a widespread explosion of executive pay and a decoupling of pay from performance, current governance practices instead give management too heavy a hand in steering the corporation. What should we do? Strengthen public laws and securities regulations, and even pursue litigation, to give shareholders a louder voice in corporate governance.

This type of argument is popular but incomplete.[1] Importantly, giving shareholders a stronger say in governing corporations offers no free lunch – doing so would also change the distributional pressures on corporate revenues and thus fundamentally alter other stakeholders' incentives to act productively. Bond market participants, for example, may demand higher interest rates to compensate for the increased likelihood of corporations pursuing projects that favor equity over debt holders. And those who are asked to instead supply human capital, like individuals in the market for managerial talent, may demand insurance measures to offset the increased risk of having their firm-specific efforts exploited by shareholders.

Through channels like these, legislating, regulating, or litigating an increase in accountability to shareholders can lead to a less-productive corporation. This theoretical concern has received considerable empirical support. Scholars have found evidence, for example, that *authoritative* shareholders tend to award golden parachutes. This pattern shares a stronger consistency with shareholder democracies ultimately threatening other stakeholders than with managers indulging their own preferences when shareholders are too diffuse to productively govern the firm. And similar patterns appear in data on bond prices, as well as anti-takeover protections in initial public offerings (IPOs) - strong shareholders, not weak ones, tend to offer protections that are popularly characterized as evidence of too much managerial power.

In this light, shareholders appear to willingly tie their hands when doing so productively insulates other important stakeholders from opportunistic redistributions. Diffusing the firm's ownership, in a symmetric manner, can be a capable substitute for such commitment devices – one that raises the cost of "owner" opportunism, and

---

[1] Bainbridge (2002, p. 441) goes even further, characterizing this type of argument as "erroneous".

D. Falaschetti, *Democratic Governance and Economic Performance*, Studies in Public Choice 14, DOI 10.1007/978-0-387-78707-7_6,

can thus elicit a more productive effort from stakeholders (under certain conditions) at a lower cost than would formal hand-tying arrangements. Mandating a stronger voice from shareholders could take this choice away from private organizational strategies, risking the stability and productivity of the public corporation business form, and ultimately the economic performance to which this form has made such strong contributions.

## 6.1 Widespread Support for Increasing Accountability to Shareholders

The potential for "unaccountable" managers to weaken corporate performance has been widely observed, across both time and space. Adam Smith called attention to this problem in the 18th century, and President Franklin D. Roosevelt argued against entrenched corporate greed in his 1936 State of the Union address (Lublin and Thurm 2006, p. A16). And while contemporary calls for a more democratic governance of corporations are loud and growing stateside, they are perhaps even more forceful in Europe. Both the Democrat and Republican nominees for the President of the United States in 2008, for example, made campaign promises to require shareholder approval of executive pay packages (Say on pay in America 2008), while the Netherlands, Norway, and Sweden already give shareholders a binding vote on compensation, and the United Kingdom requires a non-binding say on pay (Pay attention 2008).[2]

Rather than reflecting a widespread interest in efficiently aligning managerial actions with shareholder interests, however, support for such policies may instead come from special interests in redistributing the corporation's product. Henry Hansmann (2000, p. 5), for example, suggested that "workplace democracy" might substitute for waning state socialism to produce a more equal distribution of wealth.[3] Viewed in this light, it is not surprising that pressures to better align corporate decisions with shareholder preferences are feeding off the argument that executives enjoy excessively high pay levels. Indeed, prominent investor advocates have argued that excessive compensation will not go away until boards of directors start serving shareholders instead of executives (e.g., see Forelle and Scannell 2006, p. C4; Lublin and Thurm 2006, p. A1).

As policy after policy failed to rein in perceived excesses, calls for a strengthening of shareholder democracies appear to be gaining support. In 1993, Congress changed the tax law so that pay in excess of $1 million could not be deducted as a business expense, unless excessive pay was tied to performance. According to Senator Charles Grassley (R-IA, and former chair of the Senate Finance Committee), the goal of this reform was to stop the gap between executives and

[2] Iwata (2008) offered a popular review of these pressures more generally.

[3] Sowell (2008) made a related observation.

"people further down the ladder" from growing too wide (Forelle and Scannell 2006, p. C4). [4]

But rather than curb the growth of executive pay, this change may have fed it, as strong firm performance fueled a 1990's bull market, and changes in executive pay tend to track those in firm size (Gabaix and Landier 2008). Coupled with this continued increase in pay levels, a more recent scandal over the alleged ex post dating of stock options (which are often a part of performance pay packages) encouraged Congress and regulators to formally revisit the issue of executive compensation. Senator Grassley, for example, has proposed to remove the deduction of *any* excessive pay, whether or not it is tied to performance (Forelle and Scannell 2006, p. C1).

At the same time, regulators were expanding required disclosures about compensation. While legislators and activist investors attempted to rein in excesses in the early 1990s,[5] for example, the US Securities and Exchange Commission (SEC) addressed the issue by requiring firms to disclose compensation in a more uniform manner. And discouraged by the persistence of excesses to this day, the SEC recently expanded these requirements in an attempt to more transparently disclose the "total compensation" that executives receive. To that end, all statements that are filed with the Commission on or after 15 December 2006, and required to report information about executive compensation (e.g., proxy statements), must offer an enhanced set of compensation tables that include explicit valuations of performance-based pay.[6]

But while enhanced disclosures might constructively address what Lucian Bebchuk and Jesse Fried (2004) coined "camouflaged compensation", the SEC's recent actions may do little to ease demands for a more active shareholder role in corporations. On its surface, the problem of excessive compensation for Bebchuk and Fried comes from the difficulty that outsiders encounter when trying to evaluate non-salary compensation. But the root of the matter, for Bebchuk, Fried, and others, is executives enjoying too much influence over the pay-setting process itself.

According to this argument, a more effective solution would be direct ballot access for shareholders. Relative to that in other countries, shares in US public companies tend to be widely held. This diffusion, in turn, creates a free-rider problem for shareholders who want to productively govern their firm, exposing board members

---

[4]This type of motivation is also apparent in Europe. For example, Antoine Zacharias, the former chairman of French construction giant Vinci, recently lost in litigation to exercise stock options that the company had awarded him. While Vinci's performance under Zacharias was "outstanding", the weight of public opinion against "excessive pay" appears to have been overwhelming. Echoing this sentiment, prominent politicians have threatened more regulation, characterizing executive pay levels as a "social scourge" and "scandalous". And, already, the Netherlands is considering legislation that would levy additional taxes on annual salaries or severance payments above €500,000, while France is requiring severance payments to be tied to performance (Pay attention 2008).

[5]Jeffrey Gordon (1991) reviewed some of this history.

[6]Mayer et al. (2006) summarized the development of these SEC requirements.

to more forceful influence from the executive agents they are supposed to monitor than the shareholder principals whose interests they purportedly serve. To break this symbiotic relationship, Bebchuk and Fried (2004) (and others) have argued that shareholders should be given more direct access to the corporate ballot.

## 6.2 Strengthening Shareholder Democracy: Policy Developments

Given this supportive backdrop, policymakers are developing rules that would again try to make executives more accountable to shareholders. The SEC, for example, recently considered a proposal that would have allowed large, long-term shareholders to more easily propose changes to how public corporations elect directors (Bauman et al. 2007, p. 548). And while the rule was not adopted, it received considerable and high-level support. Then the SEC Chairman Christopher Cox, for example, observed during the rule's comment period that letting securities law continue to block shareholder access stands "fair corporate suffrage" on its head (Scannell 2007, p. C1). And Senators who oversee the SEC prominently supported the Chairman in this regard, observing that "shareholders are the owners of a public company and have a right to meaningfully participate in electing directors without incurring an undue cost of a separate proxy solicitation" (Dodd 2007).

Realizing that he did not have enough votes to adopt the "shareholder access proposal", Chairman Cox voted with two other Commissioners to largely exclude shareholder proposals about director elections from corporate proxy materials.[7] The Chairman reportedly saw this vote as necessary to give filers clarity about how shareholder proposals would be treated for the 2008 proxy season. He also vowed to revisit the proxy-access issue, however, when the SEC returns to its full complement of commissioners (Dorsey and Whitney 2007; Milbank et al. 2007).[8]

In the meantime, pressure continues to build for state lawmakers to revise their incorporation rules so that shareholders can more easily veto management-proposed directors. Currently, the incumbent board and its nominating committee put forward a slate of directors and, under standard procedures, each share can cast one vote on each nominee. Nominees, in turn, require a plurality of votes to formally gain

---

[7]At the time of this vote, only four of the SEC's five Commissioner seats were occupied.

[8]The 2006 opinion of the US Court of Appeals for the 2nd Circuit fueled demand for this clarification. Overturning a previous district court decision, the 2nd Circuit argued that the SEC's 1976 interpretation of Exchange Act Rule 14a-8, which allows management to exclude from corporate proxy materials any shareholder proposal that "relates to an election", does not allow an exclusion of proposals to amend corporate bylaws so that shareholder-nominated candidates would have to be added to management's slate of director nominees. Moreover, the Appeals Court argued, the SEC never rationalized subsequent changes from its 1976 position, which saw the SEC consistently take "no action" since about 1998 against exclusions of any proposal that would result in contested elections (Bauman et al. 2007, pp. 548–553).

approval (Bainbridge 2002, p. 444; Bauman et al. 2007, p. 547).[9] Under a plurality rule, however, management nominees could win an uncontested election with one affirmative vote, even if shareholders withhold a majority of their votes. Legislatures in important corporate law states, including Delaware, have thus revised their statutes to allow for majority-rule elections through shareholder amendments to bylaws and articles of incorporation (Dorsey and Whitney 2007).

## 6.3 Can Accountability to Shareholders Go Too Far?

Arguing that shareholders should have more expedient access to their companies' proxies, Arthur Levitt, Jr. (2006), former Chair of the SEC, observed that "counting every vote is not only integral to our political life, it is central to our economic life as well." But while the policies described above attempt to move in this direction, and many would like to take additional steps toward stronger shareholder democracies (e.g., requiring financial exchanges to make majority voting a listing standard), giving shareholders a more immediate say in corporate affairs creates risks for firm performance, including a destabilization of intra-firm politics and increased exposure to pressures that favor distribution over efficiency.

### *6.3.1 Shareholder Democracy Can Destabilize Business Strategy*

As proposals to change formal governance policies continue to develop, the pressure that varied interests, including pension funds, regulators, state attorneys general, hedge funds, and nongovernmental organizations, are bringing to corporate decisions appears to increase. Allan Murray (2006) thus observed that, as a consequence, boards of directors are "beginning to look more like legislative bodies, responding to the demands of disparate constituencies."

Changes like these may be facilitating a more democratic corporate governance. At the same time, however, they may also be risking the stability of intra-firm politics and thus the macroeconomic performance that relies so heavily on corporations themselves.

Social choice scholars have long appreciated the potential for this type of risk. More recently, insights from these scholars have been extended to better understand how corporate organization and law can influence economic performance.[10] An important legal feature in this regard is management's broad authority to exclude

[9]Eight states, including California, require that a "cumulative voting" procedure govern the election of directors; that is a voting mechanism that gives each share a number of votes that equals the number of director positions that are facing election (Bainbridge 2002, pp. 445–446).

[10]Late-eighteenth century philosopher, mathematician, and political scientist, Marquis de Condorect, frequently receives credit for having first formalized the potential for instability in collective decision-making mechanisms. Nobel prize-winning economist Kenneth Arrow considerably extended Condorcet's "paradox" (1951) and pushed the theory even further to better understand

shareholder proposals from being distributed through corporate proxies and thus preempt voting on any such initiatives. This restriction on "ballot access" certainly appears undemocratic, but can also bring order to the inherently unstable process of aggregating divergent shareholder preferences.[11]

To see the potential for this benefit, suppose that the management of a mining company wants to expand its operations, through an increase in either capital- or labor-intensity. Suppose also that the "increasing-capital strategy" can reasonably be expected to create more profits and less additional environmental damage than does the "increasing-labor strategy." Given these expectations, a coalition of "profit-maximizing" shareholders would prefer to increase capital rather than labor, and would prefer to increase labor rather than maintain the status quo operation.

To the extent that owning shares facilitates the pursuit of private gains (as it might with more open ballot access), however, there may also exist a strong coalition of shareholders that is more interested in labor's share of revenues than profits per se (e.g., a labor union). And given the distributional consequences of the various strategies in our example, members of the labor coalition would most prefer the strategy that increases employment. And if that alternative becomes unavailable, it would prefer the status quo operation to the labor-displacing strategy of increasing the operation's capital intensity.

Finally, the prospect of accessing the corporate ballot could also attract a coalition of shareholders that is more interested in "social values." Members of this group, in our example, are likely to prefer the status quo operation to *any* expansion of environmentally damaging mining operations, while preferring an expansion that would employ more surgically precise extraction technologies (i.e., the increasing-capital strategy) to an expansion that relied on labor-intensive methods that might create more collateral damage.

Table 6.1 summarizes these preference profiles. Notice that, to the extent that each of these shareholder blocks is large and free to access the corporate proxy, the profit maximizers might propose a vote on whether to expand operations via capital or labor, and this proposal could win with additional support from the social values coalition (which also prefers to expand capital rather than labor).

**Table 6.1** Preferences over corporate expansion strategies

| Profit | Labor | Social values |
|---|---|---|
| Increase capital | Increase labor | Maintain status quo |
| Increase labor | Maintain status quo | Increase capital |
| Maintain status quo | Increase capital | Increase labor |

decision-making in organizations such as corporations (1974). Gordon (1991) and Miller (1992) developed important positive and normative extensions for corporate law and organization.

[11] As our example below highlights, this access restriction may also discourage shareholders with divergent preferences from entering the game in the first place.

Faced with the prospect of its least-favored alternative (i.e., the increase-capital strategy), however, the labor coalition could propose an expansion of labor against the status quo. And notice that this second proposal could also win, since it draws additional support from profit maximizers.

But increasing labor in our example would add the most to environmental damage and is thus the least favored strategy of the social values block. These voters may thus access the ballot themselves, proposing to maintain the status quo rather than increase capital. And coupled with the support of labor, the members of which also prefer the status quo to increasing capital, the social values voters could see their top-ranked alternative adopted.

Rather than letting any group benefit from its most favored strategy, however, this democratic process may see all groups suffering from the consequent instability of intra-firm politics. Indeed, ease of access to the corporate proxy can attract divergent interests to the pool of "owners", and in our example lead to a cycling of votes for increasing capital over increasing labor, increasing labor over maintaining the status quo, and maintaining the status quo over increasing capital. Moreover, the potential for such instability is not an artifact of our example's simple set of choices. Rather, the message from the social choice literature is that the risk of experiencing a voting cycle increases with the number of both shareholder factions and possible operating strategies.[12]

In this light, corporations appear to be exactly the type of organization that can benefit from a concentration of decision-making authority. The problem of distributing a corporation's revenues, by its very nature, gives rise to strongly conflicting preferences; for example, after creating any level of output, each coalition wants to "split the dollar" in its favor, a preference that necessarily opposes that of all other coalitions. Confronted with such diversity, then, collective decision-making mechanisms must concentrate power or face a considerable risk of creating chaos (Schofield 1985).

Having to confront this type of "quandary" regularly creates "managerial dilemmas."[13] Importantly, the persistence of these dilemmas does not appear to come from a lack of experimentation with different organizational and legal structures. Rather, it more likely comes from the fundamental nature of collective decision-making. Consequently, while strengthening shareholder democracies may appear to be an obvious antidote to laws that now concentrate decision-making authority in boards of directors, it will encounter fundamental difficulties in attempting to live up to its promise. Indeed, the end game for such alternatives may not be a more prosperous and egalitarian set of business organizations but rather a set of more contentious firms that change strategies at opportune times to serve distributive interests rather than expand economic possibilities more generally.

---

[12] See, for example, Schofield (1985).

[13] See Schofield (2008) and Miller (1992), respectively

### 6.3.2 *Shareholder Democracy Can Put Other Stakeholders at Risk of Inefficient Takings*[14]

The relationship between shareholders and other stakeholders (e.g., managers) is frequently characterized as one in which shareholders are principals and stakeholders are agents. In this light, we often focus on mechanisms (e.g., monitoring by shareholders) that are supposed to constrain managers from playing self-interested actions that take away from firm efficiency.

However, this specification of the principal–agent problem discourages analysis of a fundamental obstacle to efficiency in the corporate organizational form – namely, the temptation for shareholders to expropriate (rather than share) the product of other stakeholders. Confronted with this prospect, other stakeholders rationally hold back on contributing individually costly inputs to team production processes. Unless shareholders can credibly commit against this type of opportunistic taking, all of the corporation's stakeholders can find themselves making due with an inferior outcome. Interestingly, corporate laws and organizational features that are oftentimes criticized as creating or exploiting a weakness in shareholder control (e.g., anti-takeover measures) may instead expand economic opportunities by strengthening this type of commitment.

#### 6.3.2.1 Democratic Corporate Governance Can Improve the Monitoring of Inputs, but Also Facilitate the Taking of Outputs

Following Armen Alchian and Harold Demsetz (1972), a common interpretation of the owner–employee relationship is one in which owners mitigate "moral hazard in teams" by actively monitoring their employees.[15] On its face, the corporate organizational form appears to give shareholders the right incentive for producing these monitoring services. Monitoring facilitates gains from team production by increasing the correlation between the productivity of a team member's input and the compensation with which firms reward those members. And as the firm's "residual claimants", shareholders have an interest in maximizing these gains.

> One method of reducing shirking is for someone to specialize as a monitor to check the input performance of team members. But who will monitor the monitor? Another constraint can be imposed on the monitor: give him title to the net earnings of the team, net of payments to other inputs . . . Specialization in monitoring plus reliance on a residual claimant status will reduce shirking (Alchian and Demsetz 1972, pp. 781–782).

---

[14] This and following sections draw from and extend Falaschetti (2002).

[15] "Team" refers to a team production process. For Alchian and Demsetz (1972), this process is one in which at least two factors (not owned by a single individual) have interdependent productivities (i.e., the marginal product of each factor depends on at least one other factor) and combine to produce some output. Moral hazard in teams arises to the extent that observing inputs is costly, since the inability to perfectly observe inputs creates an incentive for individuals to free ride off others' efforts. "If detecting such behavior were costless, neither party would have an incentive to shirk, because neither could impose the cost of his shirking on the other" (Alchian and Demsetz 1972, p. 780).

Facilitating efficiency gains, however, is not the only action with which shareholders can increase residual earnings. Rather, they also have an incentive to strategically tilt the distribution of earnings in their favor, even if that means taking a larger slice from a smaller pie. Bengt Holmstrom (1999, p. 79) thus asked "what assures that the monitor doesn't cheat on payments when performance meets the standard?" Only stakeholders who are constrained to receive a fixed share of a team's production find it optimal to pursue opportunity-expanding rather than redistributive strategies.

If the incentive for monitors to strategically manipulate the distribution of output goes unchecked, and if this incentive is common knowledge, then team members will not "enter the game" in the first place, since the product of their efforts stands a good chance of being expropriated. Reliance on residual claimant status to encourage monitors to play a productive role is not enough – a mechanism is also necessary to constrain monitors from opportunistically redistributing the team's joint product.

#### 6.3.2.2 Residual Claimants Are Well Positioned to Offer Incentive Pay Schemes, but Have Difficulty Keeping Promises

Alchian and Demsetz (1972) seminally argued that moral hazard in teams arises from the inability to perfectly observe inputs and thus the incentive for individuals to free-ride off others' efforts. But because it is prohibitively costly to measure *every* input, even monitors cannot fully extinguish free-riding. Holmstrom (1982) thus turned his attention to organizational strategies that might eliminate free-riding, even when observing inputs is prohibitively costly.

For Holmstrom, the essential efficiency-enhancing feature of separating ownership from control is not that it encourages shareholders to efficiently monitor other stakeholders. Instead, separating ownership from control creates an external agent, a "budget breaker", that can credibly penalize team members when they have no incentive to punish themselves.[16] Budget breakers implement these penalties via incentive compensation schemes that focus on output measures of performance (rather than on inputs as monitoring schemes do).

Note, however, that outputs are frequently observable only with long and variable lags. Consequently, to be feasible, budget-breaking mechanisms must rely on deferred compensation contracts.[17] But just as the incentive for external agents to cheat on payments creates a credible commitment problem for "shareholders as

[16]Holmstrom (1982) showed that any sharing rule that allocates the joint product of team members exactly among those members (i.e., a "budget-balancing" sharing rule) must induce either an inefficient equilibrium or an efficient but unstable outcome. Budget-breaking sharing rules, on the other hand, allow for punishments that are strong enough to sustain efficient outcomes, even when inputs are unobservable. Appendix 6.1 offers a more detailed summary of Holmstrom's model.

[17]"Optimal contracts between a manager and shareholders (via the board of directors) will often involve deferring compensation until better information about manager performance becomes available. These contracts will necessarily be long term and likely be implicit [given the prohibitive cost of identifying every future possibility and contingent payment]" (Knoeber 1986, 159).

monitors", so does the necessity of relying on deferred compensation contracts for "shareholders as budget breakers."

This problem arises because the optimal strategy in a deferred compensation contract is "time inconsistent" - after learning the level of output, the residual claimant has an incentive to renege on its promise to remunerate other team members for their productivity. Anticipating this endgame, rational stakeholders will curb their efforts early on, leaving the corporation's stakeholders with an inferior outcome.[18] Whether shareholders play a monitoring or a budget-breaking role, they must thus credibly commit against abusing that authority, or risk pushing their corporation into an inferior state of performance.

## 6.4 Diffuse Ownership Weakens Shareholder Democracy, but Strengthens Commitments Against Opportunism

In reviewing how shareholders might productively address team production problems, as well as the potential for shareholder opportunism to exacerbate this problem, we implicitly assumed that shareholders can easily act in concert. But what if shareholders, themselves, constitute a "team"? Then, to expropriate the product of other stakeholders, shareholders must overcome a free-rider problem of their own. And if the incentive to free-ride intensifies with team size, then diffuse shareholders will be relatively inefficient expropriators.

In this manner, forces that create the team production problem (e.g., the incentive to free-ride) can also mitigate the potential for owners to expropriate the product of other stakeholders' efforts. Rather than simply weaken shareholder democracies (as critics of corporate law have highlighted), diffusing ownership may thus also create a force for efficiency by enhancing the credibility with which shareholders can promise (explicitly or implicitly) to forego opportunistic takings. Indeed, to the extent that shareholders cannot organize to facilitate takings, they can better play the *passive* budget-breaking role that Holmstrom (1982) argued is necessary for other stakeholders to efficiently contribute to team production processes.[19]

---

[18]Moreover, notice that repeated interaction may not alleviate this credible commitment problem. First, the notion of a repeated game may be strained in this context since individual shareholders tend to be anonymous and the composition of shareholders constantly changes. The payoffs that any individual shareholder can recognize from building a reputation for cooperative dealings may thus be insignificant. In addition, while repeated interaction might sustain a cooperative outcome, it can sustain other outcomes as well. Hence, a model of equilibrium selection must accompany any reference to repeated interaction as a mechanism for producing cooperative outcomes.

[19]Consistent with this conjecture, Garvey and Gaston (1991) found evidence in a sample of Australian firms that the incidence of deferred compensation schemes increases with ownership diffusion.

## 6.5 Evidence on How Weakening Shareholder Democracy Can Improve Corporate Performance

Diffuse ownership of US corporations is prominently cited as the root cause of inefficiently weak shareholder democracies. As we have seen, however, the collective action problem that discourages diffuse owners from productively monitoring other stakeholders can also protect stakeholders from opportunistic takings. Rather than being *fundamentally* disadvantaged, then, loosely held corporations may enjoy a net advantage in addressing team production problems. And extending this logic, corporations that have concentrated shareholdings may do better by employing institutions that substitute for the credibility-enhancing role that "undemocratic" corporate governance can offer.

This section reviews evidence on how anti-takeover measures can play this role. Institutions like golden parachutes are frequently criticized as evidencing the excessive rewards that managers tend to capture when the voice of shareholders is too weak. The evidence reviewed in this section instead suggests that *strong* shareholders, not weak ones, adopt such measures. This pattern is more consistent with anti-takeover measures productively insulating stakeholders from the opportunistic pressures highlighted above than with such measures benefiting stakeholders when shareholders cannot productively govern the corporation.

To see how protections against takeovers can elicit a more productive level of stakeholder effort, consider the stylized fact that corporations tend to increase in market value on the event of becoming a takeover target. One way to interpret this tendency is that takeovers can reasonably be expected to create efficiency gains for *all* of the corporation's stakeholders. Notice, however, that it may also evidence an expected redistribution from non-shareholders to shareholders. And rather than simply being a theoretical possibility, Andrei Shleifer and Lawrence Summers (1988, pp. 36–37) have argued that the potential for such expropriations is empirically important.

> Since firms' labor costs far exceed their profits and since even poor capital investments yield some returns, very small differences in firms' success in extracting rents from workers and other corporate stakeholders are likely to be much more important in determining market value than the differences in corporate waste associated with differences in firms' volume of reinvestment. These considerations suggest that takeovers that limit managerial discretion increase the acquired firm's market value primarily by redistributing wealth from corporate stakeholders to share owners.

Charles Knoeber (1986) put a finer point on this argument, highlighting how the prospect of a hostile takeover can weaken deferred compensation contracts (the very mechanisms that appear necessary to improve corporate performance when the quality of inputs is costly to measure). Knoeber (1986, p. 160) called attention to the fact that hostile offers directly appeal to shareholders, bypassing the immediate parties to compensation agreements (i.e., boards of directors and managers). Shareholders may be less concerned than are these parties, however, about the prospect of managers being discharged after control changes hands but before managers receive a full payout of their deferred compensation.[20] Even more, shareholders have an interest in such opportunistic actions since they can share in the proceeds of dismissing relevant liabilities. This type of opportunism thus offers a rationalization of at least some of the premium that acquirers are willing to pay over pre-announcement share prices.

In this manner, shareholders' incentive to opportunistically accept tender offers can discourage other stakeholders from efficiently participating in the corporation's team production process. But when shareholders constitute a diffuse group, their ability to collectively act on this incentive may be weak, giving stakeholders some assurance that the product of their efforts will be appropriable.[21] In this light, it is shareholders with the loudest voices who appear to create the most serious risk of opportunistic taking and thus most able to benefit from offering insurance to key stakeholders against the consequences of accepting hostile takeover bids.

### *6.5.1 Strong Shareholders, Not Weak Ones, Award Golden Parachutes*

By guaranteeing the continuation of salary and other benefits after a takeover, golden parachutes can provide this type of insurance.[22] Knoeber (1986, p. 160) observed, for example, that

> The advantage to current shareholders of a firm providing golden parachutes... is that by doing so, these shareholders can assure managers that implicit deferred compensation contracts will not be reneged. Without this assurance, managers would not agree to such contracts. They would require immediate compensation that would necessitate the use of a less precise measure of manager performance and so ... less shareholder wealth. These obstructions to hostile takeovers, then, allow better contracting between manager and shareholders.

To evaluate whether golden parachutes indeed play this type of efficiency-enhancing role, we can statistically evaluate the following set of hypotheses. If

---

[20] Anup Agrawal and Knoeber (1996, p. 381) recognized that, more generally, an increased risk of takeover "makes shareholder assurances to managers less credible".

[21] Because of asymmetric tax implications, shareholders may not have homogenous preferences with respect to tender offers. Moreover, even if shareholders agree that each of them will be better off by collectively accepting a takeover offer, preference homogeneity is insufficient for resolving collective action problems (e.g., see Olson 1971). This difficulty may be particularly severe when offers are contingent on a certain percentage of shares being tendered. Shareholders thus face a team production problem themselves when attempting to opportunistically expropriate the product of their agents. This interpretation of the shareholders' problem is consistent with the observation that "bigger blocks [of shares] held by outsiders" might facilitate takeovers because "the size of these holdings would reduce the free-rider problem that could lead small shareholders to refuse to tender" (Agrawal and Knoeber 1996, p. 380).

[22] Margaret Blair and Lynn Stout (1999) argued that corporate law can also strengthen performance through such channels. Evidence developed below is consistent with golden parachutes and corporate law acting as substitute mechanisms to protect team members from opportunistic expropriation.

the cost for owners to play opportunistic actions decreases with ownership concentration, and if accepting a hostile takeover bid is an opportunistic action, then the incidence of associated hand-tying institutions should increase as ownership concentration increases. We will refer to this conjecture as the "credible commitment hypothesis."

Hypothesis (Credible Commitment): The incidence of management insulating institutions (e.g., golden parachute agreements) *increases* with ownership concentration.

The credible commitment hypothesis contrasts the conventional wisdom that management-insulating mechanisms evidence the ability of managers to privately benefit at the expense of their owner principals.[23] Such interpretations rely on the argument that, since monitoring is costly, agents can pursue strategies that enhance their own welfare, even if doing so is inconsistent with the principal's objective. Additionally, if forces associated with the team production problem become stronger as teams become more diffuse, then diffuse owners are relatively inefficient producers of monitoring services.[24] In this light, management-insulating institutions such as golden parachute agreements become more likely as ownership becomes more diffuse.[25] We will refer to this conjecture as the "shirking hypothesis."

Hypothesis (Shirking): The incidence of management-insulating institutions (e.g., golden parachute agreements) *decreases* with ownership concentration.

To formally evaluate which of these hypotheses better rationalizes the observed pattern of golden parachutes, Falaschetti (2002) looked at whether a corporation was more or less likely to maintain a golden parachute agreement with its chief executive if its shares were closely held.[26] Controlling for alternative rationalizations, this investigation produced evidence for the credible commitment hypothesis. In particular, corporations that have at least one "large" shareholder (i.e., an owner of at least 5% of outstanding shares) are statistically more likely to maintain golden parachute

[23]"At least in the United States, the financial press is filled with notions such as... 'golden parachutes,' where incumbent management provides itself with employment contracts that transfer a lot of wealth to themselves and away from the firm in the event that the firm is taken over and they are discharged" (Kreps 1990, p. 725). In addition, "those who believe in the beneficial effect of hostile tender offers on manager performance typically deplore... [golden parachutes] which discourage hostile offers... These criticisms have led to several proposals to regulate such actions ... (A)n advisory committee to the SEC has recommended... bylaws and restrictions on the use of golden parachutes" (Knoeber 1986, p. 156).

[24]"The most obvious disadvantage [of ownership diffusion] is the greater incentive for shirking by owners that results" (Demsetz and Lehn 1988, pp. 202–203).

[25]Holding other considerations constant, golden parachute agreements enhance the welfare of relevant executive managers. If they do so without also significantly benefiting shareholders, then the incidence of such agreements should increase as the ability of shareholders to block the implementation of such agreements decreases (i.e., as shareholders become more diffuse). It follows that, if the incidence of such agreements increases with shareholder concentration, then implementing or maintaining golden parachute agreements must significantly benefit shareholders. One such benefit is enhancing the ability of shareholders to credibly commit against playing opportunistic actions.

[26]This investigation drew on a sample of one hundred S&P 500 corporations from 1998.

agreements with their chief executives than are corporations that are more loosely held. And in addition to being statistically significant, this relationship appears to be economically important. Conditioned on having at least one large shareholder (and holding other considerations constant), for example, the probability of a corporation maintaining a golden parachute is estimated to be almost 90%. Conditioned instead on having no large shareholders, the probability of maintaining a parachute agreement falls to almost 30%.

In addition, Falaschetti (2002) reported that Delaware-incorporated firms were significantly less likely to maintain golden parachute agreements, a relationship that also appears consistent with the credible commitment hypothesis. Delaware's corporate law may discourage takeover activity and would thus substitute for the "insurance" benefits that a golden parachute agreement might create.[27] Takeover activity may be relatively costly in Delaware since, for example, the state's case law allows boards of directors to cite the welfare of non-shareholder stakeholders in attempting to resist a hostile tender offer (Blair and Stout 1999, p. 308). Indeed, stock market reaction to such case law is consistent with Delaware managers having an increased ability to resist takeovers even when doing so can disadvantage target shareholders (Kamma et al. 1988). And while other states may have enacted anti-takeover laws before Delaware, "Delaware's case law precedent arguably has made hostile takeovers more difficult. State anti-takeover laws, for example, face the risk of being declared unconstitutional while Delaware case law on takeovers has a firmer constitutional basis" (Netter and Poulsen 1989, p. 32).

If external agents produce monitoring services, and if golden parachutes are evidence of management shirking, then the incidence of these institutions should decrease as monitoring becomes stronger. But the above-described relationships between golden parachutes and either the existence of a large shareholder or incorporation in Delaware oppose with this conjecture – why would the incidence of shirking increase with the availability of monitoring services? Instead, these estimates suggest that if shareholders play a productive monitoring role, then their capacity to produce such services must be offset by formal institutions that constrain them from also acting opportunistically.

On the other hand, if shareholders are better characterized as producing budget-breaking governance services, then the empirical relationships reviewed above are consistent with what we expect to observe. Budget-breakers implement compensation schemes that are functions of observed outputs. Recall, however, that because outputs are frequently observed with long and variable lags, a budget-breaker's optimal strategy is time inconsistent – agreements that appear mutually beneficial to start appear sub-optimal when the time comes to fulfill important promises. Hence, to avoid inferior outcomes, a check is necessary on the capacity for budget-breakers to strategically exploit changes in their bargaining position vis-à-vis other

[27]This conjecture is consistent with Blair and Stout's (1999) broader point that corporate law's constraint on shareholder activism enhances efficiency by creating a system in which residual-claimants can credibly commit to uphold implicit contracts.

stakeholders (changes that occur, for example, in the event of a hostile offer). Because the value of this check increases with the ability of budget-breakers to pursue opportunistic redistributions, the incidence of golden parachutes should be higher where shareholders are relatively concentrated (i.e., in firms that have a large shareholder) and where substitute checks are unavailable (i.e., in firms incorporated outside of Delaware).

### 6.5.2 *Bondholders Demand Compensation for Risks from Strong Shareholder Rights*

Managers are not the only stakeholders who might balk at a strengthening of shareholder control. Bondholders, too, have reason for concern, and evidence of this concern has appeared in a tendency for bond prices to decrease with increases in the prospect of shareholder opportunism.

Similar to the one developed above for golden parachutes, this evidence builds on the potential for corporate takeovers to facilitate wealth transfers between different stakeholders, rather than expand economic opportunities in general. Mark Klock et al. (2005) observed, for example, that while premiums that tend to be paid for acquired firms can increase the target's net worth (and thus reduce credit risks for bondholders), takeovers can also harm bondholder interests by, say, encouraging a recapitalization that heightens the prospect of financial distress. Through these channels, takeovers can create less upside potential than downside risk for bondholders.

Consistent with this characterization of how weighty are the competing forces on bondholder value, Matthew Billett et al. (2004) found evidence that holders of non-investment-grade bonds benefit from acquisitions, but not holders of investment-grade bonds. The idea here is that the marginal "net worth" benefit is considerable for holders of non-investment-grade securities while the marginal increase in distress costs is likely to be much smaller than what investment-grade bondholders experience. Results from Klock et al. (2005) further support this hypothesis, suggesting that an increase in shareholder rights significantly increases a corporation's cost of debt financing.[28]

### 6.5.3 *Value-Maximizing Venture Capitalists Also Protect Against Strong Shareholders*

Our argument so far has been that, while giving shareholders a greater voice in corporate matters may mitigate managerial agency problems, it also risks a destabilization of intra-firm politics and facilitates opportunistic wealth transfers from

[28] Klock et al. (2005) measure shareholder rights with an index of corporate institutions that strengthen the ability of target shareholders to accept hostile takeover bids.

other stakeholders. We have also reviewed evidence that both managers and bondholders demand safeguards (e.g., golden parachutes) or compensation (e.g., higher interest rates) in return for exposing themselves to such risks. Taken together, the theory and evidence suggest that corporate performance may substantially suffer from a mandated expansion of shareholder democracy, even if shareholders benefit themselves.

This suggestion finds additional support from how IPOs tend to be structured. Notice that IPOs have relatively little history that might impede them from exploring superior organizational structures, and the capable principals have strong incentives to pursue strategies that create (rather than transfer) value. Yet, even here, we regularly see the adoption of organizational features that restrict rather than strengthen the voice of shareholders.

Robert Daines and Michael Klausner (2001), for example, found evidence that anti-takeover provisions are common in IPO charters. If the stakeholders in going public do better by maximizing the IPO's price, then this relationship would appear inconsistent with the hypothesis that anti-takeover measures evidence managers' ability to enjoy rents at the expense of weak shareholders. Instead, Daines and Klausner argued, this relationship appears more consistent with anti-takeover measures maximizing value by insuring against shareholder opportunism in situations where the potential for managerial shirking is relatively small.

## 6.6 Quandaries in Macro- and Micro-governance

Norman Schofield (2008 and elsewhere) highlighted the ubiquitous nature of constitutional "quandaries" - collective choice situations where every alternative exhibits very unattractive features. In particular, orderly democracies can only emerge from relatively homogenous constituent preferences, and concentrations of political power are necessary for stability when those underlying preferences are more diverse. Democracy is not a dominant political strategy.

We encountered a qualitatively similar quandary at a more micro-level of governance in this chapter. In particular, while a more open access to the corporate proxy has been applauded for its democratic features, we saw how a consequent increase in stakeholder diversity can also destabilize business strategies. Even more, we saw how a relatively homogenous set of shareholders can find it difficult to credibly commit to contracts that would encourage other stakeholders to optimally employ their efforts on the firm's behalf.

In both cases, institutions that appear undemocratic on their face can serve an efficiency-enhancing role and thus ultimately contribute to a stronger macroeconomic performance. State laws and agency regulations that restrict access to the corporate proxy, for example, can dissuade special interests from obtaining equity stakes in firms and thus promote a relatively homogenous interest amongst shareholders to maximize profit. And among these homogenous interests, organizational and institutional features such as diffuse ownership and anti-takeover measures can provide other stakeholders with the necessary confidence that their efforts will not be exploited. While features like these are regularly criticized in popular and academic media, then, they may instead play a foundational role in letting governance mechanisms, big and small, encourage a stable and productive business environment.

## Appendix 1: Formal Overview of Holmstrom's Result

Holmstrom (1982) formally examined a team production system in which input choices are unobservable and transformed to outputs without error (i.e., the production technology is non-stochastic). In this system, non-cooperative behavior induces inefficient outcomes when joint output is allocated exactly among a team's members. Only by introducing a *passive* "budget-breaker" can such outcomes be avoided. Holmstrom thus argued that a residual claimant's essential role is *not* one of monitoring. To see this conclusion, consider the following formalization of the team production problem.[29]

Suppose the joint actions of a team's members produce an outcome $x$: $A \rightarrow R$ where $A$ denotes the Cartesian product of each agent $i$'s action choice $a_i$, $i = 1, \ldots, n$, and $R$ the set of real numbers. Holmstrom asked whether a sharing rule $s_i(x) \geq 0$ can distribute the joint product of each individual's effort (i.e., $x$) exactly among the team members (i.e., such that the rule is budget-balancing or $\Sigma_i\ s_i(x) = x\ \forall\ x$) and induce a Pareto efficient equilibrium. The answer to this question is no – *any* budget-balanced sharing rule cannot induce an outcome that simultaneously satisfies the conditions of Nash equilibrium and Pareto efficiency.

For a sharing rule to induce a Nash equilibrium, it must elicit a set of actions from which no player has an incentive to unilaterally deviate. If each player's objective is to maximize $s_i(x(a)) - v_i(a_i)$ where $a \in A$ and $v_i$ is an increasing function and denotes the cost to individual $i$ of playing action $a_i$, then the condition $\partial s_i/\partial x \cdot \partial x/\partial a - \partial v_i/\partial a_i = 0$ must be satisfied $\forall\ i$ in a Nash equilibrium. Additionally, if the set of actions that induces a Pareto optimal outcome is defined by the argument $a^* \in A$ that maximizes $x(a) - \Sigma_i\ v_i(a_i)$, then $\partial x/\partial a - \partial v_i/\partial a_i$ must equal zero in a Pareto optimal outcome when evaluated at $a^*$. Combining these two conditions, it follows that an efficient equilibrium must satisfy $\partial s_i/\partial x = 1$ for each individual, that is, the sharing rule must allocate all of (and only) the marginal product of an individual's effort to that individual.[30]

But a budget-balanced sharing rule cannot satisfy this condition. This impossibility follows from the imperfect observation of inputs. When inputs are costly to observe, individuals can hide behind the efforts of others[31] and thus command "informational rents" (i.e., remuneration in *excess* of their marginal products). A sharing rule that pays such rents, however, must break the budget.

[29]This formalization summarizes Holmstrom(1982, pp. 326–327).

[30]This implication assumes that that there are externalities in production (i.e., $\partial x/\partial a_i \neq 0$).

[31]"Since all agents cannot be penalized sufficiently for a deviation in the outcome, some agent always has an incentive to capitalize on this control deficiency" (Holmstrom 1982, p. 327).

The contrapositive of Holmstrom's result is that if a sharing rule induces an efficient equilibrium, then it must "break the budget." Breaking the budget makes feasible a class of group punishment sharing rules that induce efficient outcomes by making each individual pivotal in the sense that if any one shirks, then no one gets paid. Relaxing the budget-balancing constraint permits group penalties that are sufficient to "police all agents' behavior" (Holmstrom 1982, p. 327). Hence, for Holmstrom (1982, p. 328), the primary role of external owners is to administer incentive schemes that police agents in a credible way (as opposed to actively supplying monitoring services).

## Appendix 2: Golden Parachute Agreement for Ameren Corporation

Under the Ameren Corporation Change of Control Severance Plan, designated officers of Ameren and its subsidiaries, including current officers of the Company named in the Summary Compensation Table, are entitled to receive severance benefits if their employment is terminated under certain circumstances within 3 years after a "change of control." A "change of control" occurs, in general, if (i) any individual, entity or group acquires 20% or more of the outstanding Common Stock of Ameren or of the combined voting power of the 16 outstanding voting securities of Ameren; (ii) individuals who, as of the effective date of the Plan, constitute the Board of Directors of Ameren or who have been approved by a majority of the Board cease for any reason to constitute a majority of the Board; or (iii) Ameren enters into certain business combinations, unless certain requirements are met regarding continuing ownership of the outstanding Common Stock and voting securities of Ameren and the membership of its Board of Directors.[32]

Severance benefits are based upon a severance period of 2 or 3 years, depending on the officer's position. An officer entitled to severance will receive the following: (a) salary and unpaid vacation pay through the date of termination, (b) a pro rata bonus for the year of termination, and base salary and bonus for the severance period; (c) continued employee welfare benefits for the severance period; (d) a cash payment equal to the actuarial value of the additional benefits the officer would have received under Ameren's qualified and supplemental retirement plans if employed for the severance period; (e) up to $30,000 for the cost of outplacement services; and (f) reimbursement for any excise tax imposed on such benefits as excess payments under the Internal Revenue Code.

[32]Source: Ameren Corporation's 1998 proxy statement filed with the SEC and available at *http://www.sec.gov*.

## References


Agrawal, Anup and Charles R. Knoeber (1996). Firm performance and mechanisms to control agency problems between managers and shareholders. *Journal of Financial and Quantitative Analysis* 31, 377–397.

Alchian, Armen A. and Harold Demsetz (1972). Production, information costs, and economic organization. *American Economic Review* 62(5), 777–795.

Arrow, Kenneth J. (1951). *Social Choice and Individual Values*. New Haven and London: Yale University Press.

Arrow, Kenneth J. (1974). *The Limits of Organization*. New York and London: W. W. Norton.

Bainbridge, Stephen M. (2002). *Corporation Law and Economics*. New York: Foundation Press.

Bauman, Jeffrey D., Alan R. Palmiter, and Frank Partnoy (2007). *Corporations Law and Policy: Materials and Problems*, 6th edition. St. Paul, MN: Thomson West

Bebchuk, Lucian and Jesse Fried (2004). *Pay Without Performance: The Unfulfilled Promise of Executive Compensation*. Cambridge and London: Harvard University Press.

Billett, Matthew T., Tao-Hsien Dolly King, and David C. Mauer (2004). Bondholder wealth effects in mergers and acquisitions: new evidence from the 1980s and 1990s. *Journal of Finance* 59(1), 107–135.

Blair, Margaret M. and Lynn A. Stout (1999). A team production theory of corporate law. *Virginia Law Review* 85, 248–328.

Daines, Robert M. and Michael Klausner (2001). Do IPO charters maximize firm value? Antitakeover protections in IPOs. *Journal of Law, Economics, & Organization* 17(April), 83–120.

Demsetz, Harold and Kenneth Lehn (1988). The structure of corporate ownership: causes and consequences. In Harold Demsetz (Ed.), *Ownership, Control, and the Firm: The Organization of Economic Activity*, Volume 1 (pp. 202–222). Cambridge and Oxford: Basil Blackwell.

Dodd, Chris (2007). Dodd stands up for shareholder rights: urges Cox to reject proxy access proposal, sends letter to SEC chairman endorsing current rules. http://dodd.senate.gov/index.php?q=node/4113/. Accessed 26 November 2008.

Dorsey and Whitney (2007). Majority election of directors: where are we today? *Corporate Update*, October 25.

Falaschetti, Dino (2002). Golden parachutes: credible commitments or evidence of shirking? *Journal of Corporate Finance* 8(2),159–178.

Forelle, Charles and Kara Scannell (2006). Revisiting executive pay law: Congress may reduce, reverse deduction that fed stock-option explosion. *Wall Street Journal*, September 6, C1, C4.

Gabaix, Xavier and Augustin Landier (2008). Why has CEO pay increased so much? *Quarterly Journal of Economics* 123(1), 49–100.

Garvey, Gerald and Noel Gaston (1991). Delegation, the role of managerial discretion as a bonding device, and the enforcement of implicit contracts. In Thomas B. Fomby and George F. Rhodes, Jr. (Eds.), *Econometric Methods and Models for Industrial Organizations, Advances in Econometrics*, volume 9 (pp. 87–119). Greenwich and London: JAI Press Inc.

Gordon, Jeffrey (1991). Shareholder initiative: a social choice and game theoretic approach to corporate law. *University of Cincinnati Law Review* 60, 347–385.

Hansmann, Henry (2000). *The Ownership of Enterprise*. Cambridge, MA: Harvard University Press.

Holmstrom, Bengt (1982). Moral hazard in teams. *Bell Journal of Economics* 13(2), 324–340.

Holmstrom, Bengt (1999). The firm as a subeconomy. *Journal of Law, Economics, & Organization* 15(1), 74–102.

Iwata, Edward (2008). Corporate governance gets more transparent worldwide. *USA Today*, February 17, http://www.usatoday.com/money/companies/management/2008-02-17-corporate-governance_N.htm. Accessed 18 February 2008.

Kamma, Sreenivas, Joseph Weintrop, and Peggy Wier (1988). Investors' perceptions of the Delaware supreme court decision in Unocal v. Mesa. *Journal of Financial Economics* 20 (1–2), 419–430.

Klock, Mark S., Sattar A. Mansi, and William F. Maxwell (2005). Does corporate governance matter to bondholders? *Journal of Financial and Quantitative Analysis* 40(4), 693–719.

Knoeber, Charles R. (1986). Golden parachutes, shark repellants, and hostile tender offers. *American Economic Review* 76(1), 155–167.

Kreps, David M. (1990). *A Course in Microeconomic Theory*. Princeton: Princeton University Press.

Levitt, Arthur Jr. (2006). Stocks populi. *Wall Street Journal*, October 27, A14.

Lublin, Joann S. and Scott Thurm (2006). Behind soaring executive pay, decades of failed restraints. *Wall Street Journal*, October 12, A1 and A16.

Mayer, Brown, Rowe, & Maw (2006). SEC significantly revises executive compensation and related person disclosure requirements. *Securities Update*, August 29.

Milbank, Tweed, Hadley, & McCloy (2007). SEC amends proxy rules to permit exclusion of shareholder proposals seeking access to company proxy materials for director nominations. *Milbank Client Alert*, December 13.

Miller, Gary J. (1992). *Managerial Dilemmas: The Political Economy of Hierarchy*. Cambridge, New York, and Melbourne: Cambridge University Press.

Murray, Alan (2006). CEOs get off the ropes on executive pay. *Wall Street Journal*, July 5, A2.

Netter, Jeffry and Annette Poulsen (1989). State corporation laws and shareholders: the recent experience. *Financial Management* 18(3), 29–40.

Olson, Mancur (1971). *The Logic of Collective Action: Public Goods and the Theory of Groups*. Cambridge and London: Harvard University Press.

Pay attention (2008). *The Economist* June 14, 77–78.

Say on pay in America: fair or foul (2008). *The Economist*, June 14, 78.

Scannell, Kara (2007). SEC's Solomon? Cox splits vote on proxy access. *Wall Street Journal*, July 26, C1–C2.

Schofield, Norman J. (1985). *Social Choice and Democracy*. Berlin, Heidelberg, New York, and Tokyo: Springer-Verlag.

Schofield, Norman J. (2008). *The Political Economy of Democracy and Tyrrany*. Munich: Oldenbourg.

Shleifer, Andrei and Lawrence H. Summers (1988). Breach of trust in hostile takeovers. In Alan J. Auerbach (Ed.) *Corporate Takeovers: Causes and Consequences* (pp. 33–56). Chicago and London: University of Chicago Press.

Sowell, Thomas (2008). Ivan and Boris again: we are all Russian peasants? *National Review Online*, November 26. http://article.nationalreview.com/. Accessed 26 November 2008.

# Chapter 7
# Conclusion

## Meet the New Boss, Same As the Old Boss[1]

This book argues that, contrary to popular characterizations, democratic governance can weaken economic performance in principle and has done so in important sectors. It focuses on how democracy can go too far, not because weakly accountable politicians, regulators, and corporate executives do well when left to their own accord, but because the story of weak accountability leading to bad outcomes has been told. In other words, we are already familiar with how agency costs can diminish economic performance and appreciate how giving principals a louder voice can productively address that problem.

The punch line for this book is, simply put, strengthening that voice can, and probably does, go too far. And while it may be less popular than the conventional agency cost hypothesis, the democracy goes too far argument may not be so disagreeable. Indeed, if we appreciate that a concentration of power in our political, legal, and business agents can create problems, then it is logically consistent to think that our institutions and organizations can also give too much power to corresponding principals – voters, consumers, and shareholders. In this light, the fundamental problem becomes the "new boss" looking a lot like the "old boss" – both are more interested in distribution than efficiency.[2]

Assuming that this argument is correct, does it mean that we cannot escape from bad governance? That we are condemned to poor performance, no matter what direction we turn? The answer is "no", and hopefully this book can help us do even better in productively making the necessary trade-offs that this quandary creates.

Markets work. Adam Smith developed this insight over 200 years ago, noting that "It is not from the benevolence of the butcher, the brewer, or the baker that we can expect our dinner, but from their regard to their own interest." And Smith's early insight has stood the test of time, even receiving a mathematical proof by 20th century economists as the *First Welfare Theorem.*

So if markets just work, then where is our quandary? Can we not wind up the economy, let it go, and expect good things to happen? No. A precondition for

[1]Lyrics from the song "Won't get fooled again", by the legendary rock band, The Who.
[2]President Franklin D. Roosevelt pithily observed that "government is ourselves".

D. Falaschetti, *Democratic Governance and Economic Performance*, Studies in Public Choice 14, DOI 10.1007/978-0-387-78707-7_7,

Smith's "invisible hand" to perform so well is that individuals internalize the costs and benefits of their actions. But the extent to which individuals own their actions in this sense depends on politico-legal processes for which no invisible hand theorem exists; that is, these processes need not migrate toward mutually desired outcomes. And the social choice literature that this book lightly reviews (e.g., see Arrow 1951; Schofield 1985) shows us just how tenuous these processes can be.

The quandary, then, is buried in the background of our Chapter 1 supply and demand framework, augmented below as Fig. 7.1. We return to this starting point to neatly summarize how democratic governance can indeed put economic performance at risk, and conclude with some thoughts about the types of institutions and organizations that can mitigate this risk, and how even self-interested individuals might want to promote their development.

In a principles-level economics course, we would learn that competitive outcomes are efficient in the sense that they do not leave any mutually beneficial trades on the table; that is, the invisible hand guides us to outcomes like $Q^*$ and $P^*$ in Fig. 7.1, rather than leave us with deadweight losses like we saw in Chapter 1. To achieve such an outcome, however, we must assume that foundational politico-legal processes have succeeded in creating a low transaction cost environment (and thus encouraging individuals to fully consider the consequences of their actions). Another way to think about this book's message is that this assumption is

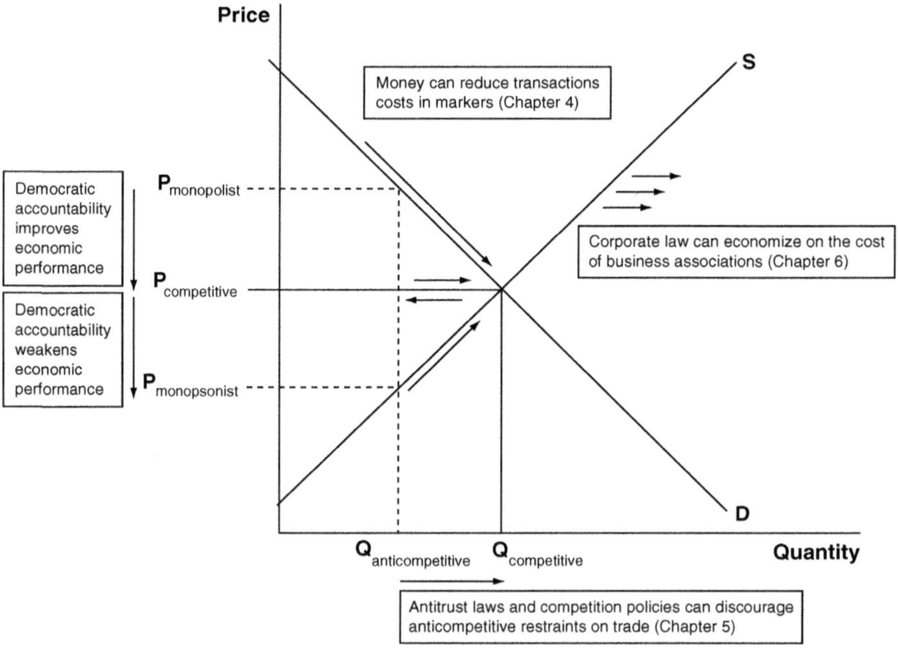


**Fig. 7.1** Democratic governance and economic performance in a simple supply and demand framework

not self-evident, and the competitive model's conclusions are sensitive to it. Indeed, we saw that forces for distribution can readily trump those for efficiency, and democratic governance mechanisms can add to the problem.

Our analysis thus suggests that striking a productive balance between distributive pressures is part of the "solution", but also an objective that is hard to fulfill. Notice, for example, that our supply and demand framework implicitly assumes a well-functioning monetary system – otherwise, how could we put price (the variable $P$) on the vertical axis? But we saw in Chapter 4 that overly accountable monetary authorities will create too much inflation, weakening money as a store of value and clouding the "real" price of goods and services that is so important for the invisible hand to work its magic. Here, "too much" democracy increases transactions costs – resources that are necessary to find suitable trading partners and measure the attributes of goods and services that are being traded – moving us away from the conditions that are necessary for markets to work.

This framework also assumes that competition law gets it right – perfectly balancing the pressures from producers and consumers. But we saw in Chapter 5 that neither constituency has an interest in efficiency; that is, producers receive more favorable distributions when prices settle above $P^*$ and consumers receive more favorable distributions when prices settle below $P^*$. Moreover, we saw that rather than creating a force for efficiency, making competition policy more democratic can weaken economic performance (e.g., create deadweight losses) to achieve distributions that favor consumers over producers.

Finally, this simple model assumes that the laws governing business associations work well. Indeed, the level at which the supply curve rests in our picture strongly influences economic performance, and depends in turn in how costly it is to organize factors of production. A familiar problem here is when managerial agents are not as careful with corporate assets as owners would be. But simply making corporate governance more democratic is not the answer. We saw evidence in Chapter 6, for example, that strong shareholders readily adopt undemocratic institutions – not because they benefit (at least directly) from increasing agency costs but because they can get a larger slice from a bigger pie by credibly insulating their agents from the prospect of opportunistic expropriation.

While democracy appears to encounter fundamental difficulties along these margins, non-market strategies at a more microlevel might help. In each of the cases reviewed above, politicians, lawyers, and managers might do better for themselves, while improving economic performance more generally, by fulfilling the role of "transaction cost entrepreneur." Fulfilling any of these professional roles requires individuals to intermediate transactions between other parties to consistently succeed for themselves. Politicians stand in the middle of voters who are transacting over public goods, for example. And lawyers regularly develop contracts to facilitate their clients' transactions with other parties, while managers regularly stand between owners of financial and human capital. In each case, intermediaries can more consistently promise net benefits to their "clients" by economizing on the resources that those clients would have used to transact on their own.

The invisible hand theorem tells us that society does better when intermediaries succeed in this manner (since the assumption of low transactions costs is better satisfied). But we cannot rely on intermediaries being angels to act for the greater good – after all, this book grounds itself on consistently modeling individuals, whatever role they might play, as being self-interested. Instead, the micro-incentive to innovate on reducing transactions costs may come from the ability to appropriate the greater benefits that success on this margin makes available more generally. A decrease in transactions costs not only creates new opportunities for clients, for example, but also may be shared in a manner that makes the entrepreneur better off as well.

To be sure, there is no recipe for succeeding on this margin, and impossibility theorems like that of Holmstrom (1982) may have something to say about the inherent limits on this type of strategy. This book may nevertheless be useful, however, in highlighting the standards for any such strategy and pointing out stubborn obstacles that stand in the way. It may also help scholars and professionals in policy, law, and business innovate on non-market strategies that discourage individuals from wanting to pursue a large slice of a small pie, and instead facilitate the appropriation of even greater benefits from a larger set of general opportunities.

## References

Arrow, Kenneth J. (1951). *Social Choice and Individual Values*. New Haven and London: Yale University Press.

Holmstrom, Bengt (1982). Moral hazard in teams. *Bell Journal of Economics* 13(2), 324–340.

Schofield, Norman J. (1985). *Social Choice and Democracy*. Berlin, Heidelberg, New York, and Tokyo: Springer-Verlag.

# Index

**Note**: The letter 'n' and '*f*' and 't' followed by locators denote note number, figure and table respectively

**F**

GPSR Compliance

*The European Union's (EU) General Product Safety Regulation (GPSR) is a set of rules that requires consumer products to be safe and our obligations to ensure this.*

*If you have any concerns about our products, you can contact us on ProductSafety@springernature.com*

In case Publisher is established outside the EU, the EU authorized representative is:

Springer Nature Customer Service Center GmbH
Europaplatz 3
69115 Heidelberg, Germany

**Batch number: 10837190**

Printed by Printforce, the Netherlands